The *Other Woman's Affair*

Gambling your heart & reclaiming your life
When your partner is married

Paul DePompo, Psy.D., ABPP

Misa Butsuhara, LMFT

THE OTHER WOMAN'S AFFAIR

Gambling your heart & reclaiming your life
When your partner is married

Copyright 2016 by Paul DePompo, Psy.D., ABPP
Published by CBTI of Southern California

All rights reserved.

Reproduction or translation of any part of this work beyond that permitted by Section 107 or 108 of the 1976 United States Copyright Act without the permission of the copyright owner is unlawful. Requests for permission or further information should be addressed to the Permissions Department, CBTI of Southern California.

This publication is designed to provide accurate and authoritative information in regard to the subject matter covered. It is sold with the understanding that the publisher is not engaged in rendering legal, accounting, or other professional services. If legal advice or other expert assistance is required, the services of a competent professional person should be sought.

Library of Congress Cataloging-in-Publication Data:
Library of Congress Control Number: 2015910044
CBTI of Southern California, Newport Beach, California
Illustrations by Justin Quizon

ISBN-13: 978-0996250702
1. Authorship.

Printed in the United States of America
This text is printed on acid-free paper.

To anyone in a relationship who feels cast aside.

Acknowledgements & Permissions

We would like to thank all of our research participants as well as our clients at the Infidelity Clinic who bravely shared their stories with us. Without their strength, openness, and collaboration, this book would not have been possible.

It is also important that we thank our colleagues at the Cognitive Behavioral Therapy Institute of Southern California, whose dedication towards using a scientific approach with clients continues to inspire us to become better mental health professionals. We also would like to thank those at the Institute who took on more work with patience and generosity in order for us to (attempt to) meet our timelines for this self-help endeavor.

We are grateful to Dr. Windy Dryden, whose teachings have influenced the underpinnings of our work, and to Dr. Janis Abrahms Spring, whose work with couples has contributed to raising our interest and concern for the "other."

A special thanks must go to the wise Christopher Nelson, whose expertise and knowledge in poker (and most other things) have helped deepen the metaphors between poker (a gambling game of skill) and the skill required to navigate a relationship with a married partner. His graciousness in providing his insights has been invaluable.

We would also like to thank Alliant International University for assisting with the IRB process for the study. And finally, thank you, Starbucks and various other Southern California coffee houses for hosting us during our book writing during times we wanted to leave the office and feel like we were not working ... while we were.

TABLE OF CONTENTS:

STEP ONE: *Scanning the Deck & Learning from Those You Play With* *1*

    Chapter 1: Your Situation *3*

    Chapter 2: His Situation *13*

    Chapter 3: "How Did I Get Here?" *31*

STEP TWO: *Gambling Your Heart - Should You Walk Away with What You Have or Go All In?* *47*

    Chapter 4: Playing Your Cards Right *49*

    Chapter 5: Tolerating the Uncertainty *63*

    Chapter 6: Taking Life Off-Hold *77*

    Chapter 7: Putting Yourself Out There *87*

STEP THREE: *It's a Long-Run Game* *105*

    Chapter 8: Keeping You on Track – Seeing the Big Picture ... *107*

    Chapter 9: Facing Avoidance *117*

    Chapter 10: Maintaining Your Focus *135*

    Chapter 11: Knowing When to Hold 'Em *145*

    Chapter 12: Knowing When to Fold 'Em *153*

STEP FOUR: *Final Round - Putting Uncertainty in the Past* *161*

    Chapter 13: Moving on Together *163*

    Chapter 14: Moving on Apart *173*

    Chapter 15: Letting Go and Moving Forward *183*

Afterword *195*

References *197*

Resources *201*

STEP ONE

Scanning the Deck & Learning from Those You Play With

1

Your Situation

Your Hand & His Hand

Are you in a relationship with "the one"? Is he married or somehow tied to someone else? If so, you are experiencing one of the most difficult struggles someone can face. You may spend much of your time wondering how this relationship will work out. "What is his life like when he is away?" "What is he up to?" You might be asking yourself these questions while telling yourself that you're fine!

Has he told you that he and his wife are no longer having sex? Or that they sleep in separate bedrooms and they are close to getting divorced? Do you need more answers? Are you waiting to see if he will choose you instead of his wife and family?

You are probably experiencing *many* feelings and thoughts about your relationship. You wonder whether it will work out. Despite the close connection between both of you, situations come up that trigger problems.

Take 35 year-old Maria for example. She reconnected online with her high school sweetheart, Daniel. He had initially told Maria that he'd be divorced within one year. Maria and Daniel have been together for three years now. Maria is still unsure if Daniel has officially filed for divorce. At this point, Maria is really worried about the future of her relationship. She tells herself, "I've already invested three years of my life into this relationship, it *has* to work out!"

Maria's heart races and she feels nauseous throughout the day. She finds herself distracted at work as a Physician's Assistant. She worries about her relationship when she should be focused on treating patients. As a way of coping with her anxiety, Maria blocks out her thoughts about what might happen in the future. She wants to avoid conflict between herself and Daniel in order to keep things positive.

As Maria tries to just ignore her anxiety, she finds herself feeling more anxious! This becomes a cycle for her.

Take a look at the list of common reactions below. Are any of these feelings and thoughts familiar to you in your current situation? This list is a collection of some of the most common reactions we have discovered in our research and clinical work.

Common Reactions When Your Partner Is Married:

My Mood	Thoughts I Have	My Body	Things I Do
Anxious	This *has* to work out, nobody compares to him.	Tightness, nausea, racing heartbeat	Question, push away (avoid conflict)
Depressed	I *should* be enough for him. I'm not good enough.	Low energy, shutting down	Cry, isolate, avoid, sleep excessively
Angry	He *should* be treating me fairly.	Clenched jaw, flushed face, racing heartbeat	Yell, become mean, accuse
Confused	If he knows we are perfect together, why won't he leave her?	Fuzzy thinking, tense, tight, headaches	Worry, question, avoid, distract, unable to concentrate
Guilty	I'm awful for getting so upset with him.	Low energy, fatigue, butterflies in stomach	Beat myself up, beg for forgiveness
Jealous	He shouldn't be spending special time with her.	Racing heartbeat, flushed face, clenched jaw	Investigate, give the 3rd degree, act mean

If you have any of the reactions above, it's no wonder! It's human nature. The more important something is to you (like your relationship), the more *intensely* you will think, such as Maria's thought, "This *has* to work out!" This hurts your ability to think things through *clearly* and make confident decisions. Ultimately, you may be acting in ways that work *against* you in this relationship. For example, you might be hiding your true feelings or yelling when you're angry.

Is there a difference between the expectations you have about what he *should* be doing and what you are *actually getting*? On one hand, you may have a strong need to push down your worries when things are going well. You don't want to "upset the apple cart." On the other hand, you may have a stronger need to *see progress in your relationship. You feel as though you need answers and reassurance from him.*

Good Intentions

Regardless of how you are handling things, you are doing so for *good reasons*! Unfortunately, the way you are handling things may be problematic. Do you push your worries aside in order to pretend you are "fine"? Or, do you force your partner to talk about "difficult" subjects, believing dirty laundry must *always* be aired?

You may believe that confronting him will make him hear you so things can change faster. However, being confronting leads to more arguing and feeling *even more disconnected.* In the long run, nothing really gets resolved!

Despite how "stuck" you might feel, we know that your partner has many good qualities! That is why you were drawn to him in the first place! When things are going well, you see him as having the qualities you *want* in a man. You connect with him in a different way than you have with other men. This connection leads you to experience life as more fulfilling and full of possibilities. It's as if the sun shines brighter, the trees look greener, and all seems right in the world. At these times, you likely see yourself as more complete, confident, and alive. You may even see the people *around you* as more interesting and kind.

He, in turn, is very connected and attracted to you as well! However, he is also still connected to his wife through children, obligations, or a shared history. The times when he is unavailable and you *need* him are the most difficult. Having to spend holidays without him is particularly difficult. His day-to-day obligations to his family and work also take time away from you. During these times, you may experience life as lonely and dark. You may feel as though you are "in limbo," putting your life on hold, waiting to see what happens. You may see yourself as alone and secretly question your value. The people *around you* may seem unfair and selfish.

Eventually, life will need to be simplified and decisions will need to be made. (*Even no decision is still a decision; we will get into this later*). Each of your decisions will likely not be easy ones to make.

Your good intentions also shine through in what we call your "double-sided traits." Your wonderful qualities may actually be some of the <u>same qualities</u> *that make it difficult for you to navigate this relationship*. In other words, your positive traits may be working against you at times. These are qualities that you like about yourself and that *he loves about you*. (Some examples might be: your passionate personality and your understanding nature). Take a look at the table below. It highlights the ways some of your positive traits can potentially be getting in your way. We took these examples from our study participants and past clients.

Double-Sided Traits: Your Positive Traits & How They Work Against You

Positive trait:	Passionate
How It Works Against you:	Difficulty letting go of an argument.
Positive trait:	Understanding
How It Works Against you:	Difficulty getting your needs met.
	Putting others first, hoping you're next.
Positive trait:	Strong-willed.
How It Works Against you:	Losing control during arguments.
	Beating yourself up when things don't go as planned.
Positive trait:	Motivated
How It Works Against you:	Stubbornly refusing to "fail."

These "double-sided traits" can also be applied to your partner. The wonderful things that you love about him (and that he may even love about himself) may be the same traits that make it difficult for him to *make a decision or follow through*. (For example: he is nice, popular, charming, responsible, and successful). These traits can work *against what you want in the relationship*.

Double-Sided Traits: His Positive Traits & How They Work Against You

Positive trait:	Nice/Well-liked
How It Works Against you:	Doesn't want to hurt "her or the kids." Cares about what others think.
Positive trait:	Charming/Intelligent
How It Works Against you:	Ability to "say the right things" in order to avoid conflict. Influences the people around him.
Positive trait:	Responsible
How It Works Against you:	Concerned with obligation and doing "the right thing."
Positive trait:	Successful
How It Works Against you:	Fearful of declining financially or socially if he leaves his wife.

As you can see, your and your partner's traits are double-sided! They can be good or bad. You both may have good intentions while also experiencing difficulty solving relationship problems. For example, both of you may desire to be together and for the relationship to be simpler yet both of you may struggle with communicating or agreeing on a plan to move things forward.

Even when it seems like so much is out of your hands, there are many aspects of this relationship that *are* in your control. Despite the way events between the two of you unfold, this book is designed to help you navigate this double-edged relationship in which you are in love with someone who seems like your perfect match – while at the same time he is tied to someone else.

What Is This Book About?

This book is about learning to take control over your journey and living a more fulfilling, happy life, *regardless* of whether your partner stays with you and your relationship progresses, he returns to his wife, *or things between you and him stay the same.*

Why Was This Book Written?

This book is a culmination of our research and extensive work with clients in all aspects of affairs. Our work has led us to develop a helpful program to assist you in making difficult and emotional decisions with confidence *and* be the best "you" in the relationship so that it can have the best chance to succeed. Also, we have learned to spot the "ifs" and "whens" it may be time to let go and how best to do so.

We interviewed and assessed dozens of women and men who were in a relationship with a married person in order to understand their experience. We have used our research to develop emotional and practical methods to help you to either: a) increase the chances of making the relationship work or b) feel confident and stand strong if it is time to move on.

Society as a whole and the media often blame the other woman within the love triangle, portraying her as mentally unstable, oversexed, and having no morals. There is rarely any responsibility placed upon the married partner for his actions.

Even in the field of self-help books for those who have been impacted by an affair, the majority of books are written to help the couple repair their relationship while leaving the other woman out of the picture entirely. Moreover, if the relationship doesn't work out, the married partner often has his family to go back to, whether he is able to work on his marriage or not. More often than not, the other woman is left to sort out the pieces *alone* and may be isolated on a deeper level, due to not having told friends or family about this "taboo" relationship. *Additionally, there has been no clinical psychological research on the struggles of the other woman regardless of the extra-marital affair being one of the oldest relationship dynamics in history.*

What Makes This Book Different?

The good news is that *we are the first clinicians* who have researched the helpful and not-so-helpful effects this relationship is having on your life. We have devised a scientific method of helping you to overcome the anxiety and the "ups and downs" of your experience.

We guide you as you move forward now regardless of the outcome of your relationship.

We will not tell you that being in this relationship is "wrong." We would have to figure that out together; it very well may be "right." We will *not* shame you for being in this situation, as other so-called "self-help" authors have done. We understand that you feel a strong connection to your partner and wish for this relationship to work out. We are *not* writing from a "hurt" or "angry" perspective pitting you *against* your partner. We use cutting-edge methods to be a combination of the following: a supportive friend who provides you with helpful feedback, supports you, and accepts that you have good intentions and only want what is best; as well as a relationship specialist who acts as your consultant, using the most current science to help you in your situation.

How Will This Book Help You?

Specifically, this book will begin by helping you look at the things that contributed to the start of the relationship and how early life events may have lead you to your present situation. Our research has revealed several factors that bring couples together. We will shed light on why you may not have "fallen into love" but rather have walked into this difficult situation based off of earlier childhood experiences that were out of your control.

Following the exercises in this book will help you evaluate the current options that *are* in your control. We will look at how to best handle the relationship now while balancing intimacy, closeness, and an ability to move things forward. We will also teach you tools to help get your mood and emotions under control so that you can navigate this relationship (or move on from this relationship) in a healthy, productive, and empowered way that makes sense to you.

You will also develop a plan to take control and move forward in your *life*. Anxiety is a central part of this relationship dynamic and we will assist you in getting your worries under control as well.

We will strengthen your 'muscle' for being able to tolerate *the unknown*. Being worried about the future is a common aspect to this type of relationship. You and the life you want has been "on hold," not knowing what the outcome of this relationship will be.

Currently, you may believe that worrying about how things will unfold helps you because it keeps you "on guard" to things that may go wrong. We have found that increasing your ability to handle any of the possible outcomes will allow you to have more enjoyment, confidence, and an ability to be free of unhealthy worry.

We will assist you in taking your life "off hold." You can still enjoy your life and develop and accomplish personal goals despite the "hold" you are experiencing in this relationship. Taking into consideration all of the people we have researched and helped through this process, we understand that the primary concerns are for you to: make decisions you will feel confident about, do what you can to make this relationship work, and make sure that you can stay strong during this process, without behaving in ways that you may regret later.

Here is the 4- step game plan of what we will unfold in this book:

Step 1: Understanding the stakes of the "game."

- What this relationship is doing to you (*both good and bad*).

- What your partner is going through.

- Looking at how you got here. Learning the ways early life experiences have shaped your relationship (*and what to do about it*).

Step 2: Resolving your uncertainty and anxiety. Learning tools to explore what's best for you.

- Developing clear relationship goals.

~Coping with the uncertainty of what will (*or will not*) happen.

Step 3: Taking life "off hold." Learning how to enjoy life even while in limbo.

~Creating balance in your life.

~Communication techniques that really work.

~Tackling the avoidance that may be holding you back.

~Re-evaluating your relationship now that you have been working the program.

~Viewing the red flags that still may be present in your relationship.

Step 4: Being able to move forward either with or without him.

~Moving on successfully together or apart.

~Preventing insanity: "history repeating itself"

Are you ready to take the first steps in reclaiming your life? Let's do this!

2

His Situation

"He tells me he has never felt so connected to anyone before. He was the first one to say 'I love you.' But still, I don't know what he is going to do!" - Jennifer

How He Got Here

Married people who have affairs tend to have many problems in their relationships. Typically, the spouse has no clue how bad the problems really are. Growing up, they likely didn't see their parents' marriage as intimate and close. Some learned that they must *avoid* problems at all costs. Or that they must *secretly* meet their own needs to be strong. Often, they believed that cheating is something that "men do" and should be *accepted*. One should "look the other way."

Regardless of your partner's family experiences, there are commonly four "types" of men who stray outside their marriages.

Mr. Charming

Mr. Charming is smart, fun, exciting, and should only be around such people (at least, this is what he tells himself)! He truly believes he is deserving of something new and exciting. As long as it is "under-the-radar," he believes he should be rewarded for the good things he has done. He believes he should have what he wants and accepting any less would make him a fool. He thrives off the ego-boost of being adored and showing off his sexual prowess.

Though he may be of any age, many men in this category are in their 40s to 50s. They want to affirm (usually with younger partners) that they've still got it! He sees himself as motivated and an expert in many areas. Overall, he is quite charming and likeable in social situations.

Growing Up: There are two prominent ideas about why Mr. Charming might think he is so deserving. The first idea comes from the notion that Mr. Charming was very much indulged as a child. In this family, he was led to believe that he was special and entitled to special treatment.

The other idea, which is the more commonly held idea within the field of psychology, is that Mr. Charming was emotionally neglected or deprived of nurturance while growing up. Though he likely would not reveal this, the insecurity hides beneath his façade of super-confidence. Still today he is starving for attention and validation. Buried deep behind the smile, Mr. Charming struggles with his sense of worth. He secretly feels quite inferior. Therefore, he masks his feelings of inadequacy with a false bravado of confidence.

Beliefs That Developed:

As discussed in Chapter 1, we all develop a belief system at a young age. It's based on our upbringing, personal experiences, and how we connected to our parents. Within the belief system, there are "rules" that we live by. We are not always aware of these rules, such as the cliché "Things I Learned in Kindergarten" concept. Rather, these rules hide out in the background and pull the strings in our daily behavior. They form the play-book for the reasons why we do what we do!

Mr. Charming has developed his set of rules that justify his sometimes self-serving behavior. Below is a list of common beliefs that Mr. Charming has developed from childhood.

Authors' Note: *Remember, people aren't always aware of the beliefs and rules that guide their behavior. At times, these thoughts lurk in the background of their actions.*

Mr. Charming's Belief System:

- Because I am special, I should have what I want. If I deny myself, then I am losing out.

- If I take what I want and deserve, then I am strong. If I do not, then I am weak.

- If I blame others for my problems, I will be confident. If I focus on my part of the problem, I will be taken advantage of.

- If it looks good from the outside, then I am successful and confident. If I reveal my true worries and vulnerability, I will be disrespected and disregarded.

- If I can attract a younger woman, I am sexy and desirable. If not, I am getting old and losing value.

Go-To Behaviors That Help Him Cope:

Everyone uses coping skills that help him or her get through life. They are used to handle big, life-changing events and smaller, daily life hassles. Whether the coping skills are healthy or unhealthy, over time, they become automatic, "go-to" behavior. The following is a list of some common go-to behaviors that Mr. Charming may rely upon.

Mr. Charming's Go-To Behaviors:

- Busy with his pursuits: work, children, and friends.

- Lacks real empathy when you're let down.

- Focusing on his own personal gratification.

- Having a relationship with a younger woman in order to feel masculine and sexy.

- Using alcohol or drugs to improve mood, relax, or sleep.

- Spending money lavishly on himself or others.

- Finding fault in others when problems occur.

Mr. Lonely & Hurt

Mr. Lonely and Hurt lacks a connection to his wife and desires validation from someone else. His wife is demanding and he wants nothing more than to avoid conflict with her! Mr. Lonely also has a strong need for appreciation which he doesn't believe he is getting enough of. At home, he feels he gets the short end of the stick.

The unexpressed hurt has made him grow apart from his spouse. He considers the pros and cons of staying in the marriage. But currently he is *more* focused on healing his hurt and experiencing his connection with you.

Growing Up: When Mr. Lonely was a child, he learned that his own needs didn't matter as much as others' in the family. Learning that conflict should be avoided at all costs he has tolerated many hurtful situations. It is likely he may have even witnessed his own parent struggle through a difficult marriage, suffering in silence, grinning and bearing through emotional, physical, or substance abuse.

Beliefs That Developed:

Mr. Lonely's belief system is complicated. It helps him to manage his hurt, while also doing damage control to any drama at home. Below is a list of common beliefs that Mr. Lonely practices.

Mr. Lonely's Belief System:

- If I keep my hurt to myself, I will be responsible and feel good. If I asserted my needs, I would be selfish and feel bad.

- If I put others' needs first, I am strong; if I assert my needs, I am weak.

- If I avoid telling my wife (and kids), they won't be hurt and angry, and things won't get out of control. If I tell my wife (and kids), they will be hurt and angry, and things will get out of control.

- If I get my needs met, then I can handle being at home; if I do not get my needs met, I may get too hurt or angry and I will feel worse.

Go-To Behaviors That Help Him Cope:

The go-to coping skills deployed by Mr. Lonely are two-fold. They combine avoidance of talking confidently about what he *really* wants, while sneaking in ways to meet his own needs. See the list below of Mr. Lonely's go-tos that help him with his life's hassles.

Mr. Lonely's Go-To Behaviors:

- Avoiding expressing needs and wants.

- Putting others first (at an eventual cost of secret resentment).

- Distracting from connecting with partner via TV, porn, surfing the internet, or time with friends.

- Passive aggressive comments and behaviors towards others.

- Focusing on the children over his spouse.

- Over-working in order to stay away from home.

- Playing the "martyr" role to get sympathy from others.

Mr. Deprived

Years of sexual frustration in Mr. Deprived's relationship make him want to stray even though he and his wife may be good friends. His sexual self-esteem is hurting and he believes he is missing out on an important part of his happiness. He may have sexual fantasies that he cannot share with his spouse because she is just not interested or would put him down.

Though there are aspects to his marriage that may work well, Mr. Deprived feels a deep sense of pain about the sexual problems in his marriage. Work and child rearing have likely made it worse. This makes even more of a rift between he and his spouse. There are many types of sexual dysfunction that may exist in his marriage. Among the most common are the following: his wife may experience low desire, pain during intercourse, difficulty achieving orgasm (which may lead him to feel like less of a man); or he may have married young and he now believes he has "missed out."

Half of women and a third of men experience sexual difficulties. Additionally, he and his wife may have sexual drives that do not match. Troubled sex can lead to their difficulties being close. When these problems lead Mr. Deprived to not feel desired or cared for, he often goes outside the marriage.

Growing Up: Mr. Deprived can exist in any marriage, regardless of the individual histories of those involved. However, at the core of sexual dissatisfaction between spouses often lies a tendency to *avoid dealing with problems*. This could be due to shame, guilt, or general discomfort about handling sex problems.

It's possible that, similarly to Mr. Lonely, Mr. Deprived was led to feel as though his needs didn't matter. He had also not learned how to communicate confidently in order to get his needs met. Growing up, he might have learned to avoid problems if he saw his family doing the same. His family may have simply ignored, brushed under the rug, and never brought up problems in family discussions. Therefore, at this time, it's easier for him to avoid the problem entirely at home and pretend it doesn't exist.

Beliefs That Developed:

The belief system of Mr. Deprived is complicated. It is employed to avoid feelings of shame associated with the sexual problems in his marriage. It also relates to not wanting to upset his partner and guilt about having unmet needs. See the list below of commonly held beliefs of Mr. Deprived.

Mr. Deprived's Belief System:

- If I tolerate my sexual dissatisfaction, I will be a good husband. If I express my sexual desires and fantasies, I am selfish.

- If I get my sexual needs met, I will feel better and more relaxed. If I don't get my sexual needs met, I may get more depressed.

- If I am not having good sex, then I will be less of a man. If I can have good sex, then I am a desirable man.

- If I can make a woman feel good during sex, then I am a real man. If I cannot, I am not a real man.

Go-To Behaviors That Help Him Cope:

Mr. Deprived uses go-to behaviors that help him cope with feelings of shame and inadequacy. At times, he may even avoid dealing with these feelings entirely by distracting himself to an extreme.

Mr. Deprived's Go-To Behaviors:

- Avoiding expressing sexual needs and avoiding talking about sexual issues.

- Distracting self with porn, drinking, and/or overworking.

- Becoming hyper religious and focused upon religious beliefs in order to minimize the importance of sex.

- Being flirtatious with women.

- Making frequent sexual jokes and comments.

- Sleeping in separate bedroom, keeping distance from spouse.

Mr. Ready

Mr. Ready is done and ready to move on with you! Regardless of the problems within his marriage, he has truly lost hope that things can improve. Mr. Ready does not believe that loving feelings can return. Even if they could, he would not want them to!

In addition, he accepts the losses that would incur from divorce. He has considered the financial and parenting adjustments and is at peace with them. There is no confusion here; he is entering into an action plan and moving on.

Growing up: Mr. Ready may have experienced a variety of childhood upbringings, challenges, and situations. Rather than a "common" childhood that ties the Mr. Readys of the world together, one might say that lessons have been learned from his past and are now being applied to his current situation. For example, if Mr. Ready grew up in an environment with an absent father and a harsh, critical mother, he may have told himself, "I don't want to be in the same type of marriage that my parents had. I want a good, healthy relationship. I want to be with a kind, caring woman. I want to prioritize quality time together."

He may have married someone believing "opposites attract"! Now, he realizes that someone more *like* him (the good friend) would *truly* be his best match. Although people tell themselves that they will do things differently than their parents had, they often end up in similar situations. Mr. Ready has realized too many "red flags" have gone up in his marriage and he must move on, in order to avoid repeating the mistakes of the past.

Beliefs That Developed:

Mr. Ready's beliefs about relationships are relatively well-adjusted and realistic to his current situation. He may have held out the hope that his marriage would improve with time or couples therapy. They are in different places in life. Things have run their course. Therefore, at this point in time, his belief system is operating on the assumption that he will be moving on. See the list below of Mr. Ready's beliefs.

Mr. Ready's Belief System:

- If I move on, then I can grow and be healthy. If I keep hoping for different results, then I will be foolish because the relationship ran its course.

- If I attend to my needs, I will be healthy and achieve more happiness. If I continue to ignore my own needs, then I will continue to feel stuck.

- If I start to make steps towards divorce, then I will be moving forward and feel better. If I avoid taking steps toward divorce, I will be stagnant and nothing will change.

- If I focus on the healthy reasons to move on, I will stay strong; if I focus solely on the losses, I will stay stuck in fear and avoid change.

- If I talk to my partner about my feelings, then we can try to work to make sure these problems don't repeat themselves. If I keep my feelings to myself, I will repeat the past and nothing will change.

Go-To Behaviors That Help Him Cope:

Mr. Ready tries using coping skills that are positive and help him move forward. At times, he may be quite stressed about his situation. He is not doubtful of his decision; he is in reality and grieving the consequences of divorce such as financial, real estate, and child custody decisions. Take a look below at the some of the ways Mr. Ready is coping with his situation.

Mr. Ready's Go-To Behaviors:

- Financial planning for his future.

- Taking steps to handle assets to make sure he will be financially secure.

- Talking with his close friends and family about his plans and obtaining guidance and advice.

- Meeting with an attorney, mediator, and/or financial advisor.

- Going for individual therapy to sort out his feelings.

- Sleeping in a separate bedroom, using a different bathroom (when possible), etc.

- Taking clear steps to move out: apartment searching, etc.

Let's Re-Cap

You've learned quite a bit about the different "types" of men who have relationships outside of their marriages! We have bullet-pointed the main characteristics of these men below. Take another look at the four men. Ask yourself which "type" your partner currently fits into.

Check off all the traits that fit your partner. Further down below, you can jot down more traits you've noticed about your partner that we haven't already mentioned. Surely, some of these categories may cross over. Many men might be a combination of types.

For example, he may be a blend of Mr. Deprived and Mr. Lonely (i.e., DeLonely). He might be avoiding putting a plan into action because he's preoccupied with how the family would respond. At the same time, he finds comfort in the connection he has with you.

<u>Mr. Charming:</u>

- o Busy with his pursuits: work, children, and friends. He lacks real empathy when you are let down.

- o Focusing on his own personal gratification.

- o Showing you off in order to feel masculine and sexy.

- o Using alcohol or drugs to improve mood, relax, or sleep.

- o Spending money lavishly on himself or others.

- o Finding fault in others when problems occur.

- o _____

<u>Mr. Lonely & Hurt:</u>

- o Avoiding expressing needs and wants.

- o Putting others first (at an eventual cost).

- o Distracting from connecting with partner: TV, porn, surfing the internet, or time with friends.

- o Passive aggressive comments and behaviors towards others.

- o Focusing on the children over his spouse.

- o Over-working in order to stay away from home.

- o Engaging in the "martyr" role to obtain sympathy from others.

- o _____

Mr. Deprived:

- o Avoiding expressing sexual needs and avoiding talking about sexual issues.
- o Distracting self with porn, drinking, and/or overworking.
- o Becoming hyper-religious and focused upon religious beliefs in order to minimize the importance of sex.
- o Being flirtatious with women.
- o Making frequent sexual jokes and comments.
- o Sleeping in separate bedroom, keeping distance from spouse.
- o _____

Mr. Ready:

- o Financial planning for his future.
- o Taking steps to protect assets to make sure he will be financially secure.
- o Talking with his close friends and family about his plans and obtaining guidance and advice.
- o Meeting with an attorney, mediator, and/or financial advisor.
- o Going for individual therapy to sort out his feelings.
- o Sleeping in a separate bedroom, using a different bathroom (when possible), etc.

o Taking clear steps to move out, apartment searching, etc.

o _____

Additional behaviors my partner does that concern me:

_____
_____
_____
_____

When you review the behaviors that concern you and that you don't quite understand, what "types" do you think they could be categorized under? Do your best to fill them in. Again, the behaviors may fit more than one "type."

Don't Fret!

Now, if your partner is not Mr. Ready, don't fret! Mr. Ready is in a place in his relationship in which he has the goal to move on and be healthy. He is further along in his decision-making process. We cannot at this point assume that your partner is not on the "Mr. Ready track." Nonetheless, we *can* help you determine where he is at during this process, which we will revisit when you've moved further along in this program.

Until then, it's important to remember that you are now with him for good reasons. What we mean by this is that there are *distinct reasons* why you are staying in the relationship despite the fact that he is still connected to another. The bond that you experience with him *is* real for you despite the fact this is a challenging stage in your relationship.

You might be ambivalent about how to proceed. "How should I navigate this stage of our relationship?" "How long should I stay in?" "How do I know when it's time to let go?" Before we discuss these important questions, we first recommend taking a look back at how you came to this current place in your dating world.

3

"How did I get here?"

*J*ennifer is a 33 year-old personal trainer who met 45 year-old Kevin, an IT manager, as one of her clients at the gym where she works. They had nice conversations and realized they had much in common. They began dating and Jennifer started to fall in love with Kevin almost immediately.

"Kevin has such a busy work schedule. I didn't think too much of it at first when he'd rarely spend the night at my apartment or invite me over. He is always very caring; texting me several times a day to say he is thinking of me and being nice and affectionate when we're together. About three months into the relationship, I was really worried about the fact that I had still not been invited to Kevin's place. He then told me that he is, in fact, still married but is planning on divorcing when he feels that the time is right. We both love each other and there is such a strong connection between us, but it's a secret. How did I get here? I never thought I would be doing this."

Right Now

He is married and you love him. We have established that there are many things about him that are loveable. You are *not* crazy for this predicament! But did this relationship happen by chance or was it in the cards for you? In this chapter, we start from your beginning and look at what may have led you here.

On one hand, you feel very connected to him. On the other, it is not the most ideal situation. Many of our research study participants described feeling as though they were in a "holding pattern." Therefore, we will examine not only how you got here, but also what may be contributing to this "stuck-point."

We are going to go deep in this chapter, so hold on and stay with us! First, we look at *why* you do what you do. Then, we identify the "whats" and "hows" of getting "un-stuck."

Growing Up

Old episodes of "The Brady Bunch" and "Dawson's Creek" usually showcase nauseatingly "perfect" parenting. Problems in TV families are usually resolved in about 23-43 minutes!

In real life, of course there are no "perfect" parents. Parents tend to raise their children as they had been raised … or they vow to do the opposite! They also often have good intentions when they set out to be parents. Nonetheless, their good intentions can sometimes lead to their children developing poor relationship skills.

For example, while growing up, your parents may have wanted to be accommodating and flexible. But when you or your siblings became "difficult" (basically by just being kids), they may have become hurt and frustrated. As a result, your parents likely reacted angrily, critically, or judgmentally. Or, perhaps you had a parent who was raised in a very strict environment. He might have believed it worked in making him responsible and respectful. But when strictness was imposed on you, you may have experienced it as rigid and controlling!

Take a moment and think back to your own childhood. How would you describe your upbringing? What significant images or events come to mind? How did your family handle problems and communicate? Reflect on the ways in which your family parented (or did not parent) you.

Many of our research participants experienced a parent being (physically or emotionally) absent during important times in their development. Perhaps they were present, yet were emotionally absent due to their own struggles at the time. Examples of this would be narcissistic parents or parents who tended to avoid emotional connections. Participants reported that their parents were usually over-working, distant, or indulging in behaviors that brought them further from their own spouse. Some participants also lost a parent during their early teen years. Whether parents were absent emotionally or physically, many of the participants experienced a struggle in connecting with them.

Additionally, daughters had to work extra hard to get their parents' positive attention or approval. Many reported not feeling "accepted," especially when not meeting their parents' expectations. The female participants often reported that their parents tended to be poor listeners. This was most evident when the topic was not of interest to the parent. Many of the male participants described their relationships with their fathers as emotionally distant. They also tended to describe their mothers as harsh or critical.

My Experience with My Parents

(Circle below if you experienced or witnessed any of these significant situations while growing up):

Absent emotionally	Absent physically	Unpredictable Parents	Frequent comparing to siblings/others
Avoiding things	Raised by step-mom	Death/Loss	Strict, rigid parent(s)
Affair(s)	Raised by grandparent	Financial hardships	Domestic Violence
Critical	Verbal Abuse	Family illness	Avoiding Conflict
Alcohol or Substance issue	Physical Abuse Sexual Abuse	Frequent moving/change	Environment encouraged over-achievement

These childhood situations impact how we connect to our parents. How we connect to our parents impacts how we relate to our adult romantic partners.

How We Connect

Our "Connection" relates to the *type of bond* we have with our partners. For example, it represents our sense of security when we reach out for comfort. Or, it represents how we solve problems. How we connect in our adult romantic relationships begins early in our infant and toddler years. We often fit into one of the three connecting styles with our parents below.

3 Styles of Connecting as a Toddler:

The Confident Connection: As a toddler, you had confidence in your secure connection with your parents. Therefore, you felt comfortable "exploring the world," knowing you could come right back to them. You may have become a little upset if your parent left your sight. But you were easily soothed and happy when she returned.

The Anxious Connection: As a toddler, you often clung very close to your parent. You would have become highly upset and agitated when your parent left your side. When she returned, you would have been somewhat defiant towards her.

The Avoidant Connection: As a toddler, you held back and avoided showing too much emotional connection. You would have appeared indifferent when your parent left your sight. You did not want to show your true feelings.

When we grow and enter into adult romantic relationships, we repeat these patterns.

Confidently Connected adults often say: *"I find it pretty easy to get close to others. I am comfortable depending on them and having them depend on me. I don't worry about being abandoned or about someone getting too close to me."* These people often find attentiveness, warmth, and sensitivity as the most "attractive" partner qualities.

Anxiously Connected adults often say: *"He seems reluctant to get as close to me as I would like. I worry a lot that he doesn't really love me. I want us to be close but that seems to pull him further away."*

Avoidant Connected adults often say: *"I am somewhat uncomfortable being too close. Sometimes I think distance is good because it's difficult for me to trust people (although I wish I could). I don't like to depend on anyone. My partner wants me to be more intimate than I feel comfortable being."*

Remember Jennifer? Jennifer grew up as an only child with a very critical single mother. Jennifer would see her father every few years. He was mostly uninvolved and had a separate family. He would promise Jennifer that he would call her and take her to movies but would rarely follow through. She found herself feeling frequently hurt and disappointed by both parents throughout her childhood and teen years. As a result of these relationships, Jennifer developed an Anxious Connection.

Our Ways of "Acting"

In relationships, many of us try to act Confidently Connected to our romantic partners. We instinctually know it is "healthy" to do this. Yet, when problems arise, our earlier experiences can lead us to become Anxious or Avoidant.

We also use "go-to" strategies that help us cope with the conflicts in our relationships. Below, we will examine how we act when problems occur.

My Go-Tos That Help Me Cope

Think for a moment about your relationship and the last argument that occurred. You likely felt hurt, anxious, and/or angry during that situation. How did you cope with it at the time? Do you still do the same things to cope with your stress about your relationship?

Check any of the following go-to strategies that you have used, brainstorm others you have done, and write them in below. We will need this later.

Anxious Connection:

[ ] Trying to be more of what he wants.

[ ] Biting my tongue when I really want to know what's going on.

[ ] "Walking on eggshells," not wanting to upset the applecart.

[ ] On alert regarding what is happening with him.

[ ] Cross-examining him when I get worried.

[ ] Hyper-focusing on problems in order to "fix" them immediately.

[ ] Investigating to look for information about what he is doing when I am not around.

[ ] Worrying excessively about whether the relationship will work out.

[ ] Blaming myself for the lack of progression in the relationship.

Avoidant Connection:

[ ] Acting "as if" I am fine.

[ ] Calling myself "single."

[ ] Seeing other people on the side.

[ ] Using alcohol, marijuana, or prescription drugs to cope with feelings.

[ ] On hyper-alert for untrustworthy behaviors.

[ ] Avoiding discussions about the future so as not to appear "needy."

[ ] Accepting what he tells me as the "truth" when I think a good friend might tell me otherwise.

[ ] Justifying his or my behavior in my mind while overlooking important pieces that would otherwise be uncomfortable to acknowledge.

Additional Go-To Strategies I Use:

_____

_____

_____

_____

I Do It For Good Reasons

You are resilient. Regardless of your childhood upbringing and connecting style, your experience with your parents led you to develop "rules" that kept you "safe." Many people apply those "rules" from childhood to their romantic relationships. We will show you exactly what we mean as you read along.

Jennifer's Example: The "Rules" That Keep Jennifer Safe in Her Relationship with Kevin:

At this point in her relationship with Kevin, Jennifer feels quite anxious. She wonders, "Will Kevin really be there for me?" She recalls being frequently abandoned by her father: "I barely ever saw him, he was always with his new family. Maybe once every five years he would come see me or take me out. He'd promise to see me more and then I wouldn't hear from him again for another five years. I remember spending a lot of time picking out my outfit before I would see him to make sure I looked nice."

Jennifer now finds herself anxiously on alert for problems. She cross-examines Kevin when she becomes worried about the relationship. Her goal is to make her relationship with Kevin "work." Jennifer is operating based on the "rules" she learned when she was very young in order to keep herself "safe" with Kevin.

If I focus on what we need to fix in our relationship,

Then we can improve things and be closer,

And I will feel good.

If I don't focus on what needs to be fixed,
Then we won't improve things and be closer,
And I will feel <u>anxious</u>.

Jennifer has good intentions. She thinks she is being proactive in her relationship with Kevin. Unfortunately, the unintended costs are the worrying and anxious feeling, which bring more stress into her relationship.

Linda's Example: The "Rules" That Keep Linda Safe in Her Relationship with Michael:

Linda is a 42 year-old sales executive for a pharmaceutical company. She has been involved in a serious relationship with a 56 year-old cardiologist named Michael. Early on in their relationship, Linda knew he was unhappily married. She told herself she was fine with this arrangement; she never wanted to be "tied down." To her own surprise, Linda now finds herself wanting to be prioritized by Michael. She can't help but crave more time from him. Secretly, she wants to be "chosen" by him.

Growing up, Linda had her share of challenges. She was the eldest of four children in a traditional Italian-American household. Linda fell into the role of the "responsible assistant" to her mother. She describes her mother as strict and critical while her father was warm and friendly. Linda was close to her father. It was common knowledge in the family that Linda's father was unfaithful. Still, it was never questioned or discussed. She went through a difficult time at age 16 when her father passed away.

Linda keeps her worries to herself. She acts "as if" she is strong, to not push Michael away. Not wanting to get hurt by Michael, she keeps him at a bit of a distance. Still, she "has fun" when they are together.

If I keep things to myself when I am upset,
Then we can stay together and have a chance of working out
And I will feel good.

If I don't keep things to myself,
Then he will pull away, and it may not work out,
And I will feel depressed.

Linda has good intentions. She wants to make for a nice time when they are together. The unintended costs for Linda are excessive worry about how things will work out in the future. Also, she avoids having important discussions about the relationship. See Diagram on the next page for an overview of the ways that attachment, go-to behaviors, and rules interact.

Let's revisit two of the go-to behaviors you identified in the checklist above. Look at the ones that you know are unhealthy and would like to improve. Take **two** of those behaviors that you wrote down and put them into this format below. Really see what comes to mind. There are no right or wrong answers:

Identifying My Go-To Behaviors:

Go-to Behavior 1:

*If I (insert go-to behavior)*_____

Then, *(insert what will happen)* _____

And I will feel: _____

If I don't (insert the same go-to behavior) _____

Then, (insert what will happen) _____

And I will feel: _____

Go-to Behavior 2:

If I (insert go-to behavior) _____

Then, (insert what will happen) _____

And I will feel: _____

If I don't (insert the same go-to behavior) _____

Then, (insert what will happen) _____

And I will feel: _____

The Costs

Can you see? You do have good intentions behind what you do. But what about the costs? In the big picture, do these go-to strategies help you both move closer? Do they hurt the relationship? Do they make good sense given the relationship you *really* want to be having? The following are a list of the common rules and beliefs that we have found:

Common "other-woman" rules and beliefs:

> "He should be with me during the holidays. If he isn't, then it must mean that I'm not good enough and I would feel depressed. If he would prioritize me at important times, then that would mean that I am good enough and I would feel happy."

> "If I get him to talk about his feelings, then we can be close and work things out, and we will be happy. If I don't get him to talk about his feelings, he will keep them in and nothing will change, and we will be unhappy."

These rules and beliefs lead you to be motivated to *push for open communication*. The *costs* of these rules are anxiety or depression *when they are violated*. When you're alone or he seems closed up, it may trigger you. You then may act in ways that push him further away. As a result, you feel even more alone.

> *If I push him too much, then he will go away, and all this will have been for nothing, and I will be depressed. If I stay patient, he will still be around, and he will know that I really understand him, and we will be happy.*

> *If I trust completely, then I may get hurt and feel like a sucker. If I don't trust completely, then I will be safer, and not feel dumb if this doesn't work out.*

These rules and beliefs may lead you to be very motivated to "*keep things cool.*" They are geared to hold back problems and protect you. You hope things will eventually work, so you want to keep the "good image."

Often, the *costs* of these rules are feelings of anxiety or depression *when they are violated*. When you're alone, you may act out in ways that bring you further apart. You may call an old boyfriend or engage in some other indulgent behavior. This may let you excuse his behavior, getting him off the hook. The end result? No real change.

When he is nice and loving, you may not be able to let him in. Here, there are many costs. You may be so "on-alert" to protect yourself that you may not open up. You may not hold him accountable enough to see where this relationship is going. He may see your behavior as "handling it okay" with no need for change!

Revising Your Rules

As an infant, you first learned to lift your head. Then, you advanced to crawling, standing, walking, running, biking, and driving. As you evolve, the things that once worked for you may no longer work. Especially not in the healthier life you are trying to achieve! Today, some of your rules will still work for you. Other rules will not and will require an upgrade!

Navigating Your GPS

We started by sharing how events from your childhood influence the way you connect with your partner. How you connect determines your go-to strategies. Finally, we discussed the "rules" and beliefs that keep you stuck in a strategy. Though well-intended, these rules can have costs to you and the relationship.

In the next chapter, we'll help you identify or perhaps take a fresh look at your goals in order to explore how you want to handle the relationship going forward. This may entail developing some new or revised rules, which will lead to new behaviors. New behaviors will help you get unstuck, moving you in the direction to have the type of relationship you desire!

STEP TWO

Wagering Your Heart – Should You Walk Away with What You Have or Go All In?

4

Playing Your Cards Right:

Getting your head and your heart in the game

Goal Development

We have discussed in detail your current situation. We have examined the likely "type" of man you are in love with. We have also looked at the significant events of your past that led you to this place. Now we are going to start getting into the meat and potatoes of our work together!

It is important to first develop *goals for your relationship*. The goals should take into account both what is important to you *now* as well as what you anticipate will be important to you in the future. As a teen, did you already picture your "grown up" relationship? Did you imagine yourself getting married and/or having children? Your ideas and desires may have changed since then. Or, they may have stayed pretty well the same. We ask you to reflect upon what is important to you *now*. Where do you want this relationship to go? We will help you on your path to getting there.

Goals vs. Desires

It's no wonder that goal-focused people report psychological well-being and satisfaction in their lives. Some people have goals to exercise more, be a better friend, or be more productive. Most people identify "relational goals" as getting married or having a family. But, if these ideas are *not* put into action, they are merely *desires*, not goals. Desires can be excellent starting points for developing goals – but they are *not* goals themselves. Once we put them down on paper and *take steps* to accomplish them, then they become our goals. In this way, they have a better likelihood of being achieved.

The good thing about setting and sticking to goals is that they produce *direct* changes in our relationships. They can also provide *indirect* changes in those around us (our partners)! This is a comforting relief! We can only change our *own* behavior and not that of others. But, we can often *indirectly* change others' behavior when we change *our own*! Changing our patterns in our significant relationship changes the relationship itself. This is important in moving the relationship forward.

Transforming Desires to Goals - Starting with Desires

Let's do an exercise to help you get started transforming your desires into goals. Read through the passage below before completing the written portion:

Exercise:

Imagine your relationship being exactly the way you want it to be. Take a minute, close your eyes, and just dream. What do you see? Where are you? How does it feel? Who is there? Are you inside or outside? What are you wearing? If music is playing in the background, what is it? Listen for it. What are you feeling? How do you feel in your body? Does someone you know have this type of relationship? *(*Really stop to consider this.)*

Now jot down some of the most important pieces of those images, thoughts, and feelings that you would *want* in this relationship. There are no right or wrong answers here.

The most significant images, thoughts, and feelings when I dream of this relationship are:

Images I see: _____

Thoughts I experience: _____

Feelings I feel: _____

We had Linda do this exercise as well:

Images I see: *I see Michael and I on the patio of our house. We are sharing a nice bottle of wine. I hear the song, "Can't Take My Eyes Off of You." It is summer and our friends have gathered. It is 4th of July at our home. There are chili pepper lights outside, we have a barbecue going, and we're having fun.*

Thoughts I experience: *I am right where I want to be. It is okay to slow down and take everyone and everything in.*

Feelings I feel: *I feel warm and light. I feel joy. I feel free. I feel strong and connected to everything. I am at peace.*

Moving To Relationship Goals

While reflecting back on these desires, how can you transform them into *goals*? Now that your creativity has been ignited, what are some goals you want in your romantic relationship? What goals would have to be in place for the image you described to come true? For example, are you living with or without your partner?

You needn't consult with your partner on the formation of your goals. These are things that are important to you with *whoever* you will be in an intimate relationship. *These items are only goals if they are IN *your* control. They are not goals if they are dependent on *his* current state. These goals relate to what you *value* and want in your life both *short and long-term*.

Authors' Note: *Once you develop your short-list of goals, put them in your phone or a place where you will see them constantly. This will ensure they're in the front of your mind!*

Later, we will discuss the ways that you can take small steps on these goals. This may entail sharing these goals with your partner. See the list below for examples of some specific starting-off goals. When achieved, they can help you gain focus in getting the relationship you desire.

Linda's initial list of relationship goals:

1. In a monogamous relationship, eventually cohabitating.

2. Dating in a relationship that is free, involving our friends and family.

3. A relationship in which we prioritize each other (with time and holidays, etc.)

4. Creating a home together.

5. Planning the future together, i.e., getting engaged.

Your initial list of relationship goals for the relationship that you want:

1. _____
2. _____
3. _____
4. _____
5. _____

Debriefing Your Goals

While looking over your list, you can probably imagine there will be some road blocks. This can be the case with any list of goals! Working to achieve them may be a *challenge*, yet very worthwhile in the long run!

You may be uncertain *whether his current desires are actually goals that you both share.* As we have discussed earlier, he may have the best of intentions. However, he may not be in a place where he is willing to *prioritize his desires*. His behavior changes will remain to be seen as you work through this program. Making small, positive steps will lead to bigger ones! The changes you make will *directly* impact you (and are likely to *indirectly* impact him).

After looking at your relationship goals, you may be unsure about whether wagering your heart is a good investment. After all, there are many risks and potential consequences of doing so. If you are unsure about moving forward with your partner, please read the next section on "Getting Off the Fence." Otherwise, you may skip forward to the section entitled "Cool Under Fire."

Getting Off the Fence

Are you feeling uncertain about whether you want to continue in this relationship? If so, you are "on the fence," stuck between two possible sides, where the grass is green on both. Being on the fence keeps you very conflicted. Some have described this feeling by saying, "I either want this whole situation to just go away or I don't want to be the one to make any decisions, period."

The fence can be very tricky. It can trick you into thinking that it is *empowering* you by making you *casually wait* to "see what happens *naturally*." However, it may potentially keep you away from your goals. You could end up sitting on the fence for years, detoured from the life you desire. Getting off the fence is a process that gets you back on track.

Let's explore the ways that staying on the fence affects your thoughts, feelings, and behaviors. Suppose you have the following thoughts: "I don't know what to do. On the one hand, I have invested so much into this relationship and I don't want to leave. On the other hand, I am not so sure that staying is a good idea." These very thoughts may lead to a sense of apathy, helplessness, and a lack of energy and motivation. In turn, you can end up feeling quite depressed and anxious. And how might you *behave* while feeling depressed or anxious? You might withdraw, isolate yourself, or avoid friends and family. As in a circular fashion, these very behaviors lead to *even more* feelings of sadness, depression, and anxiety.

A more in-depth example of this can be seen with Linda. When Linda first began dating Michael, she thought she could "handle it." She shared, "A part of me always knew that he probably wouldn't leave his wife and I was okay with that. I wanted to live my own life anyway. I never wanted to be tied down by a man."

However, over time, Linda grows more hurt by the barriers between Michael and herself. "It's really hard when he can't be there for me when I need him. Holidays are painful. *We* should be together on those days."

At this point, Linda is so stuck on the fence that she wants Michael to *indirectly make the decision for her.* "I almost wish he would just mess up in a big way, you know? Like, if he just *really hurt me*, it would be so much *easier* for me to leave him. I guess I'm *waiting and seeing* what will happen."

As you can see, Linda has a good intention. (Avoiding dealing with her ambivalence head-on.) But this comes with a cost. (Having little control about her situation by "waiting and seeing.")

By "waiting and seeing," you may be giving your partner the sense that all is good; the coast is clear; it is smooth sailing and clear skies. In turn, without a crossroads or conflict, your partner may believe it's all about *him* navigating his difficult situation. He may fail to realize that a true relationship takes into consideration his *and* your happiness.

Getting off the fence could be a top short-term goal to tackle. You can now ask yourself, *"What more information do I need to know in order to believe it's worth it to invest more of my heart and time in this man?"*

Let's also point out that intentionally *not making a decision at this point is still a decision*! As long as you're *aware* that this is the path you're choosing, you will feel better because you are *choosing* it. You might decide that "waiting and seeing" for a *set amount of time* is a good option for you. You can incorporate the tools you learn from this program and see *how he responds*. The information and exercises we present are designed to better prepare you to handle your evolving situation.

At this point, let's survey your options. To be blunt, it seems you have *three main choices*. You can: 1. Choose to stay in this relationship *as it is*; 2. Choose to stay in this relationship while making efforts to move forward *with your partner*; or 3. You can move on from this relationship altogether. There may be times when you think these choices are *all his to make*. However, that is *not the case here*. You can still decide what *you* want even if his ideas don't match up with yours.

A Step To Getting Off the Fence

Many big decisions are difficult to make because each side has its pros and cons. You may have written a pros and cons list before. However, we encourage you to write a "weighted" pros and cons list for staying versus leaving your relationship. The difference here is that we use a scale from 1 to 10 to rate how *important* each pro and con is to you. This is useful because it helps you focus on the *values* that are important to you in your relationship. Otherwise, your list would probably come up even on all sides. You would end up feeling even more confused!

For example, suppose you end up with a list that is heavy on pros. Some pros will be more important to you than others. By rating, you give a specific value to each one. It is important to exhaust *all possible pros and cons*. Take a look at the Table below of Linda's 4-quadrant weighted pro and con list.

Linda's Weighted Pro/Con List:

Pros of Staying with Michael (1-10)		Cons of Staying with Michael (1-10)	
We have a strong physical connection.	6	I have been feeling more and more hurt.	8
He takes me out on fancy dates.	4	I often feel lonely in this relationship.	8
He buys me expensive gifts.	3	It prevents me from meeting someone else.	7
We have a lot of fun when we're together.	8	I wonder if I will ever be prioritized.	7
	Total: 21		**Total: 30**
Pros of Leaving Michael (1-10)		**Cons of Leaving Michael (1-10)**	
I will feel free and have a fresh start.	7	I will really miss him.	7
I will no longer be in pain.	8	I might be making the wrong decision.	8
I will be better able to focus on my career.	9	I might be losing a great catch.	8
I can focus on my personal goals better.	9	I could still feel lonely.	7
	Total: 33		**Total : 30**

You do not need to make a *final decision* based on this exercise. The benefits of this exercise are two-fold. First, it helps you get all of the pros and cons out of your head and onto the page. Second, it allows you to assess the differences between what your head and your heart tell you. You may *know* things logically while *feeling* different. Using the weighted pro and con list takes both logic and feelings into account.

This is not a list that you will put into *immediate action*. It will just help you to get things started. The purpose is to brainstorm the true benefits and costs of your relationship. Now fill in the blank Table on the next page with your own weighted pro and con list. Try to rack your brain and come up with 20 items for each category if possible.

Pros of Staying with My Partner (1-10)	Cons of Staying with My Partner (1-10)
Total: _____	Total: _____

Pros of Leaving My Partner (1-10)	Cons of Leaving My Partner (1-10)
Total: _____	Total: _____

Being on the fence tends to make us mentally foggy. It also leads us to procrastinate in making decisions. Getting your pros and cons organized on paper helps to clear the cloudiness.

*This exercise gives you a calculation of what is *logically* best for you. We understand that being logical is not the *only way* to make a decision. Besides logical decisions, people can certainly make emotional decisions too. Emotional decisions can be valid and healthy if *your mood is in a healthy place*. This takes us to our next section on staying "cool under fire."

Cool Under Fire

We're talking about "keeping your cool." Why are we bringing this up now? In a nutshell, keeping your cool is your ability to *stay calm during times of stress*. (Our usage of the word "cool" is *not to be confused* with a sense of "not caring." You can care while staying calm at the same time.)

When we get triggered in our relationships, we might feel angry and have an outburst ... and maybe even throw something across the room! When this occurs, we are *not* staying cool under fire. Staying cool under fire is a *life skill that takes practice* for anyone to master.

We bring up the notion of keeping your cool at this time because we are aware of two things: 1. We promised that we would assist you in navigating your relationship and keeping your cool is a *key part* in that endeavor; 2. This book may, at times, trigger you because we go very in-depth into our work together and we bring up sensitive issues.

Staying cool under fire helps people be their best selves in their relationships. Without this ability, people would act upon their impulses. This might be fine during a fun night out with friends but it doesn't help in building lasting relationships.

Mindfulness

One way to practice keeping your cool is by using *mindfulness*. Have you heard the buzz lately about this concept? Complete mindfulness training is outside the scope of this book. But we can give you some good tools to use in order to help you *be your best self in your relationship*.

Mindfulness is based upon Buddhist teachings. It's a practice in which you remain aware (mindful) of yourself and the things you do *while you're doing them*. Therefore, one cannot multi-task and be mindful at the same time.

You can practice being mindful right now, in this moment. Where are you? How do you feel in your body? What do your surroundings look like, sound like, smell like? Are you sipping a drink while you read? If so, how does it taste? How are you sitting? Are you comfortable and relaxed in your position? Take note of this *current moment in time*.

Being mindful helps you keep your cool. If and when your relationship triggers you, you will be *aware* of the trigger, aware of how you *feel*, and then aware of how you *respond* to the trigger. This helps you to make conscious decisions about your *own behavior*.

Part of mindfulness is also simply *allowing* a feeling to occur without struggling with it. You let the feeling come and go. That is what feelings do; they come and go like waves. Even strong emotions such as anger don't last in full blast for more than a few minutes at a time. Mindfulness allows you to experience an emotion as it is. There is no urgency to change the emotion or force it away.

In life, it's a given that we all experience negative emotions from time to time. We must learn to tolerate them. It's in our best interest to avoid acting out impulsively, despite the fire we feel in the moment. As you continue to read this book, we will help you build upon your strengths in order to make all these concepts easier to apply.

Summary

Whew, you did a lot in this chapter! In brief conclusion, you first identified some of your important relationship goals. You examined the effects of "being on the fence." You wrote out a pros/cons list to help you start "getting off the fence." You also learned about the importance of "keeping your cool." Your relationship is important. Important events bring about intense emotions. *Learning to ride out the waves will keep you on track with your goals.* Next, we will discuss ways to get control over the worry that may be keeping you stuck from moving forward.

5

Tolerating the Uncertainty

"When we are just together talking and doing our thing, there is nothing better. It feels perfect for me ... the way it should ... and I try not to think about when he has to go back home to her. I know I will eventually get to that anxious place anyway." -Maria

Anxiety. Some people call it "stress," others call it "worry." Whatever you call it, it's a real bitch! It's not just *thinking* about what's going to happen in your relationship. It's really believing you *"HAVE to know"* and it *"MUST be the way that it should"* (*the both of you happily together*). You may believe you *"MUSTN'T* feel too hurt or foolish if it doesn't work out." Or, that you *"HAVE* to keep things under control." That it'd be *"AWFUL* if the relationship were to fail." You would "not be able to *tolerate* it." However, is your goal to *increase the chances of this relationship being successful?* If so, being able to stand strong regardless of the outcome and *accepting the uncertainty* are key points to the process.

There's a part of your brain that knows there are no certainties in life. The more you try to have them, the more you get yourself attacked by anxiety. You can then spiral with worry or just shut down. It's very *desirable* for him to be (or become) Mr. Ready. You'd both build a happy life together. Nonetheless, just because you and he are really connected, *doesn't* mean it *must* happen! If it was a *"have-to,"* it would just *be* … like breathing to live!

If it didn't work out, it would be "bad" because of your connection. But, it would not be the *worst* thing that could happen to you in this world (*though it might feel that way initially*). It may be *"difficult to tolerate"* a break up after all you have invested. Still, there is *no reason to think you wouldn't survive it*! (*And eventually move on.*)

You've likely proven your strength in difficult situations before. If it doesn't work out, would it be saying something negative about *you or your worth?* No! Your value is not like the stock exchange that goes up and down, depending on others' actions. Your value relates to who YOU are. All your good (and the flip side of that good) are all a part of you, regardless of him. He may decide not to honor the connection and make the two of you work. This would merely be a *choice* that he has made. A choice related to his personal priorities influenced by so many factors both in and outside of the relationship.

Padesky and Mooney are world-famous psychologists who have created an equation for anxiety. It explains what needs to be done to better manage your relationship. The (relationship) anxiety that you're experiencing connects to how dangerous you believe this situation is coupled with thinking you don't have enough coping abilities to keep your head above water: (A=D ^ /C v). This means, if you have *healthy* coping, you can gauge the true risk of hanging in. You will be able to keep your cool and bounce back with resilience. Building your coping so you can best navigate this relationship will be our focus in this next step.

The OTHER WOMAN'S AFFAIR

Remember Maria? Maria is a 35 year-old physician's assistant who was previously married. She lives with her 10 year-old daughter and 8 year-old son. Daniel was her high-school sweetheart and she has reconnected with him on social media. They live an hour plane ride away and see each other whenever Daniel comes into town for business. For over a year, they meet whenever Daniel can, but it is "not often enough." They've talked about Daniel leaving his wife and getting a place of their own with their children. They joke that they would be a modern day Brady Bunch.

As the holidays approach, Maria feels anxious about when and if this is really going to happen. After all she has invested, she believes it "*must* work out!" They desire a life with each other. Yet, the barriers between them are starting to take their toll. Daniel says that he doesn't want a divorce to damage his children. He says he will "eventually" talk to his wife and try to get her on board with separating. Maria tries to block out the uncertainty she feels and tries to focus on just enjoying their time together. This is definitely a challenge. When she's alone, she becomes anxious about where the relationship is going and finds herself worrying. Over time, Maria grows more impatient. Still, she believes she "*has to hang in!*" Otherwise, it would be "all for nothing."

Strengthening Your Coping

"What Ifs"

One of anxiety's biggest weapons *against* you and your relationship is the "What Ifs." You know what the "What Ifs" are! They're the questions that rapid-fire in your head. They happen so quickly that it's difficult to even respond! We would need a real psychic with a real crystal ball (*assuming one exists*) to know whether any of these "What Ifs" will even happen! The "What Ifs" can really spike up your anxiety. They make your body tense and on alert for disaster. They can spiral your thoughts far off into crazy-land! Of course, these reactions are not helpful to you or the relationship.

Maria has many "What Ifs" in regards to her current place in her relationship with Daniel:

- What if he never leaves his wife?

- What if my children get hurt (again, from another loss) if we break up?

- What if, *after all I have invested*, we end up breaking up and I feel like "the fool"?

Identifying Your What Ifs

Most people experience "What Ifs" throughout the day such as: "What if I win the lotto?" "What if the cashier forgets to ring in the sale price for that item?" "What if there is no parking?" And so on. For the most part, people do not deeply tune into those "What Ifs" or hyper focus on them. Those "What Ifs" come in and wash out like a wave of thought.

When something as important as our potential life partner is at stake, we tend to hyper focus on those "What Ifs." This can get quite unsettling. Some people say that the "What Ifs" impact them the most while they are with their partner. Others report that they come afterward when they are alone during the nighttime hours.

Haunted By The "What Ifs"

The "What Ifs" are such a weapon *against* you because they intrude during times of vulnerability and uncertainty. When the "What Ifs" keep coming, it can seem as though you are defenseless against them. You may try to block them out or push them away. Though, like a Chinese finger puzzle, the more you *resist* these "What Ifs," the *tighter* of a hold they have upon you. Trying not to think of them can be a well-intended tactic that can lead you to spiral.

It isn't about NOT thinking about the "What Ifs" that helps start to get them under control, but HOW to think about them. We will show you. Let's start by capturing these thoughts and writing them down. Think about the last time you were feeling stressed or anxious while focusing on your relationship. What were the "What Ifs" that were attacking you? Write them in below.

What if_____?

What if_____?

What if_____?

On a scale of 1-10 ("1" being no anxiety/stress at all and "10" being the greatest amount possible), how do you rate your anxiety after thinking of these "What Ifs"?

Rate 1-10: _____

The good news is that there is ammunition at your disposal to attack back! Your secret to winning the battle against the "What Ifs" is the development of … the "Then Whats!" As we stated earlier, building your coping skills will greatly reduce your stress and anxiety. It will improve your ability to navigate the rough terrain in your relationship. You will also be putting yourself in the best position to find out what is truly *best for you*. Also, you can execute a plan that allows you the best chances to *get what you want in the big picture*.

"Then Whats" – Developing Your Plan

Your "What Ifs" need to be held accountable. When they start firing away, you need to say, "Wait a minute!" Feel free to get *ticked off* at your "What Ifs"! Why not? They are trying to mess with you! *Slowing them down* is what will start helping you get things under control. Holding them accountable means having a plan for each of the "What Ifs." This will prevent the emotional spiraling. You will also get a firmer grip onto what you *can* control, while living *with* uncertainty (*something that we all must do all the time anyway*).

Simple (*but not always easy*), the "Then Whats" are your plan. *What would you actually do* if the "What Ifs" *really happened*? While constructing your "Then Whats," get outside of your head. Imagine a plan that you would suggest to a good friend. What if she were going through a similar situation? *It's easier to think of good advice when it's not you. We get a brain freeze when it's us.* Also, we are not even looking at whether your "What Ifs" are realistic. We are preparing a plan to hold the "What If" accountable. This will help you take more control and feel stronger.

While asking Maria to sit with the uncertainty and develop her "Then Whats" as if she was helping a friend, this is what she came up with:

What If: He never leaves her?

Then What: Then I would have to decide whether I could accept that or not. Most likely, I would break it off.

What If: My Children get hurt (again) from the loss if we break up?

Then What: Then that would be sad, but I would be there for them, and we would have each other and we'd move on.

What If: After all I have invested, we end up breaking up and I feel like "the fool?"

Then What: Then I would cry and it would be bad. I would open up to a friend or maybe even go to therapy. But I would not let myself feel like a fool. I would remember the *flip side* of feeling like a fool is that I *trusted* him and *took risks*, and those are *good things* when you are trying to have a *healthy* relationship.

As you can see, when Maria is attacked by the "What Ifs," she can fire back with the "Then Whats." While responding back to her "What Ifs," she holds them accountable. She is problem-solving and reassuring, as though she is giving advice to a close friend.

Identifying *Your* "Then Whats"

Let's look back at your "What Ifs" that you had identified above. Start by writing down the one that is most intense for you:

What if_____?

Now, suppose that happened. What would you do ... really? It is important to slow down and really think it through. What would you say to a good friend who had the same "What If"?

Various "Then Whats," Broken Down:

What would you do?

_____

How would you cope?

_____

Would you survive it?

_____

Then what would you do?

_____

How might you feel about it 6 months later?

_____

--One year later?

_____

Re-rate your anxiety/stress now on a scale of 1-10. ("1" being no anxiety/stress at all and "10" being the greatest amount possible).

Rate 1-10: _____

Has the level of anxiety/stress gone down? You have captured your "What Ifs," including your most worrisome "What If." A detailed "Then What" plan has been created. Keep this plan handy for yourself and go over it! This way, it will be there when you need it! The "What Ifs" try to sneak back in when you're vulnerable. Just like dealing with a bully, it is important for you to practice standing strong in the face of the anxious "What If." If you do so consistently, you will get stronger! The bully of the "What If" will go away!

You now have a new tool to help you be better prepared when anxiety rears its ugly head. From now on, when the "What If" bully pops up, (as it tends to do), practice holding it accountable. You can deliberately practice going to the "Then Whats." This will get easier with time the more you practice. You can even search for "What Ifs" as a daily ritual. This will make the bully go away quicker because you aren't scared anymore.

Many clients find it helpful to track their "What If" to "Then Whats" on a daily basis in their mobile phone. Some use a small journal that they keep with them and refer to as needed. This helps them to see that they are in control and cutting anxiety off at the head. In our next section, we will supersize what you are learning by discussing probabilities and certainties. This will enhance what you have learned so far about dealing with the unknown.

Probabilities V. Certainties

In the last section, we assisted you in identifying your "Then Whats" in order to develop a coping plan holding those "What-Ifs" accountable. In this section, we focus upon deepening this skill by teaching your brain to assess the *actual probability of those "What Ifs" even occurring.*

Weighing The Probabilities

In poker, there are no certainties. A good player has a combination of skill (knowing the probabilities of the cards that might turn up) and luck (the cards that actually do turn up). Navigating this relationship with its uncertainty is similar. We encourage you to examine your worries in terms of the *probabilities* of what could happen. This is more helpful than *demanding* to *know* something that only time can tell. As you know, you can't always control the outcome, but you can certainly assess probabilities and develop your plan. This true, logical, and healthy philosophy will strengthen your ability to cope while you work toward your goals.

Worst-Case Scenario

Worst-case scenarios are absolutely the most horrifying outcomes that you can imagine. When you engage in worst-case thinking, you probably believe it helps you be prepared. For example, Maria is afraid that Daniel will never leave his wife. Anxiety creeps in and convinces Maria of the worst-case scenario! "He will not leave her and I am going to stay with him anyway and feel horrible ... or, I will leave him after so much time, I won't meet anyone else!"

Here, Maria has a choice. She can *still* fight back with a "Then What," e.g.:

What if: I end up *never* leaving and never having the life with him I envisioned?

Then What: I can *choose* to set a deadline for when I vow to move on!

She may also consider:

Then What: I can work on *accepting* the choice of staying.

I can learn how to have a satisfying life when he is *and is not* available.

Or, as we propose in the next section, she can consider the "Worst – Best – and Most Realistic Scenarios."

Worst – Best – Most Realistic Scenario

Worst - Best - Most Realistic retrains your brain to focus on the *most* realistic outcome. This is done by making yourself not only look at *the Worst* – but also *the Best* and *Most Realistic*. People often believe that "imagining the worst" helps them be "prepared." As you look back in time, how often has the worst-case happened? What has the cost been of you focusing on the worst? There is too big of a price to pay when you focus on "the worst." Worst-case thinking is a poor investment. You get yourself upset *regardless* of what actually occurs!

Maria gets herself anxious by her "worst-case" thinking with Daniel. As a physician's assistant, she believes this thinking helps her at work. Nonetheless, Maria has been finding herself stressed both at home and at work.

Maria's ***worst*-case scenario** with Daniel is that she will stay stuck in the relationship and never have the "real" relationship she desires. She reports she would then never feel "good enough" and would grow to resent Daniel. Here, we challenged Maria to also not only look at this *worst* but also consider the *best* and *most realistic* scenarios in order to truly assess the possibilities:

What is the *best*-case scenario?

Maria said that the best case scenario would be that when he *says* he will *not* leave his wife, she "would be so strong, powerful, and ready to move on, that her strength would make him come to his senses and finally get the courage to leave his wife." This *is* possible, but it may not be that *likely* at this point in the game. Still, it warrants consideration.

What is the *most realistic* case scenario?

After looking at the worst and best-case scenarios, look honestly at the scenario that is *most realistic*. Maria said that most realistically, "If he says that he will *not* leave his wife, I will eventually leave the relationship. It would be a struggle, but I would be able to move forward. I have had break-ups before and although this one would feel different, I would survive it."

Moreover, she said that during that window of her healing, he *may* make changes, but if not, she would most realistically make herself move forward regardless of him. She knew that she would likely struggle with losing the traits that she loves about Daniel that may be hard to find in other men. But after mourning the loss, she believes (as she has done before), that she would be likely to find comfort trusting that the new men she chooses to date would be available for the kind of relationship she desires.

Now let's re-state the "Then What" plan *you* have developed earlier in this chapter:

What If: _____?

Then What: _____

_____

What is the *worst*-case scenario that could happen next?

_____

_____

What is the *best*-case scenario that could happen next?

_____

_____

What is the *most realistic* based off your ability to be resilient in the past?

_____

_____

_____

Summary

In this chapter, you learned how to increase your ability to cope with the unknown. By working this plan you can more effectively: 1. Navigate the crossroads in your relationship with the best of your strength and resilience; 2. Practice turning your "What Ifs" to "Then Whats;" and 3. Strengthen your ability to focus on the Most Realistic scenario. Capturing those "What Ifs" and developing plans help you cope without having to feel tortured by something that is not most realistic.

We discussed deepening this plan by developing new habits of where to focus: 1) Focusing away from the "worst case scenarios." 2) Considering the possibility of the "best case scenarios." 3) Working to reinforce the "most realistic" scenarios. Zooming in on anything else would be self-defeating as well as relationship-defeating. It would mess with your coping. It could lead you to either spiral or bury your head in the sand.

We are now set for our next chapter. The next step is to further increase your strength and coping. We will get you back to *focusing on you*! To increase your joy *regardless* of what happens with him! This next step will help you to keep growing and sharpen your confidence. You will gain important tools in order to continue navigating this relationship.

6

Taking Life Off Hold

"My lease is expiring soon and I want to move out of my place. We have talked about moving in together but by the way he has been so slow to follow through on things, it doesn't seem like it will happen any time soon. I don't know what to do." - Jennifer

Many people who want a successful relationship experience the following beliefs: *"If I put my relationship first, then things will get better. I will feel good and* then *I can focus on myself. If I don't put the relationship first, I may lose it and then I'd feel horrible."*

In relationships, as in a good investment plan, people should diversify. "Putting the relationship first" and focusing solely on that will actually hold you back. Finding balance in your day-to-day life within *yourself* and in your relationship is important. In so doing, you will actually move closer to your relationship goals. You will also experience more joy regardless of the outcome.

Putting Life on the Front Burner and Getting Balanced

Jennifer, like many women in this situation, finds herself in a holding pattern. It is challenging enough to deal with an uncertain outcome. To also be concerned with *how the outcome affects your life* is extremely stressful. Your career, family life, friendships, and children can all be affected in various ways.

Some women even miss out on career or other relationship opportunities in order to *"see what will happen."* You might also be experiencing fear of the unknown. Other women report, *"Since I have been through so much and compromised my morals, this must work!"*

The holding pattern is likely to continue with the following two factors. First, he's on the fence about closing his current chapter and starting a new one with you. Second, you focus on his positive traits instead of your relationship goals. The longer the relationship stays stagnant, the more likely you will struggle with anxious, sad, and depressed moods. The more anxious, sad, and depressed you feel, the greater the likelihood the relationship (and you) will *continue to stay stuck*.

Just as the status of your relationship affects your mood, your mood can prevent you from accomplishing your relationship goals. Your *relationship* may be in a holding pattern but YOU don't have to be! Lifting the hold will get your mood on track in a positive direction.

Your Balance

Getting yourself in solid working order will help you cope with anxiety about the outcome of your relationship. Also, it will help you move toward your relationship goals. Today, you cannot control how this relationship will turn out. But that doesn't mean *you* must be "on hold!"

There are specific ways you can improve your mood while achieving more life balance. No matter what happens, you can stay strong and move forward. Currently, the things in your control are: 1. *The type of relationship you choose to be in (or not be in)*; and 2. *How you spend your time and energy.*

Your Mood DNA

Have you ever seen crime shows such as "Dateline" or "48 Hours Mystery"? When the detectives find case-cracking DNA, they become very excited. They are unlocking the clues to the mystery!

The "clues" to the "mystery" of your mood and motivation need to be discovered. The stress of the unknowns in your relationship can hurt your mood and keep you stuck. Just as a mystery cannot solve itself, we need to take action! We cannot feel better if we *wait* to feel better or *wait* for things to change.

Finding your "mood DNA" gets you motivated to work on your goals. The secret is experimenting with what you DO. What you DO unlocks the stuck-ness in your mood and motivation.

Padesky's Five-Part Model shows this connection with the following example: if you have a goal to "feel stronger when he is with his family," and (1) you do not make weekend plans with friends or family because you are waiting to "see what happens" (your behavior), (2) you will likely feel lonely (your emotion) because you (3) will be telling yourself something to the effect of, "I am so lame for being alone on a Saturday night" (your thought). (4) You are likely to have less energy on Saturday night (your body) and (5) your home can become a lonely place (your environment).

Another course of action, when you have the same goal, would be to: 1) Push through on Wednesday to make weekend plans with a friend (your behavior). 2) During the weekend, you will likely feel more excited (your emotion) because you will be 3) telling yourself, "This is a good thing, I am taking care of myself" (the thought) and you will likely have 4) more energy and motivation (your body). As a result, 5) going out with a friend (the environment) can become a rewarding and comfortable activity.

Yet another secret to unlocking your mood is that you don't have to FEEL like it to DO it, whatever IT is! People usually decide whether or not they should do something based on how they *feel*. We advocate for the opposite! We recommend that you *start the doing even if you don't feel like it*. The "feeling like it" comes later!

How Should I Be Pushing Through?

Accomplishment, Anti-Avoidance, and Pleasurable Tasks

Three things have been proven to improve mood when done consistently. First, doing things that make one feel accomplished. Second, tackling everyday things in life that one usually avoids. Third, doing pleasurable things. When people incorporate these activities into their daily lives, their moods naturally improve.

Achieving your personal balance of these activities will give you many good days! Multiple good days will make you balanced and become habit. In turn, you become stronger, healthier, and able to move toward your goals. Taking small steps to find your balance will lead to bigger steps and bigger changes!

Accomplishment Tasks

Accomplishment tasks do not have to be amazing things. (You can get control over your mood without being a Nobel Prize winner or curing cancer). These tasks could be anything that you do to upkeep your life. It could be the act of taking the kids to school or going to work. It is the performance of the day to day "have-tos."

For example, when you are stressed or feeling down, it's even an accomplishment to get out of bed or cook a meal. When you are stressed about your relationship, it is an accomplishment to get your work done. Some people are heavily driven to be accomplishment focused while others are not. It is the balance that you need that is most important.

> *List 5 of the day-to-day accomplishments that are important for you to be maintaining on a regular basis:*

Accomplishment Tasks:

1. _____
2. _____
3. _____
4. _____
5. _____

Anti-Avoidance Tasks

We all have lists of things we avoid doing. Actually, we all have things we avoid, we just haven't gotten around to making a list of them yet! These tasks can be very basic. For example: getting more organized, scheduling time with family, exercising more consistently, going to the doctor, etc.

These tasks can also include more challenging things. For example: making important decisions that have no guarantees or putting your needs first (*at least sometimes*). Whatever it is, the act of avoiding can impact your mood and goals more than you may imagine.

When you wait to "feel" like doing a task, you are more likely to put it off even more. Avoiding important tasks leads to a decline in mood. People tend to feel stuck and even further away from their goals as a result.

Do you HAVE TO *feel* like it to start? Let's say that your child or niece was kidnapped. The only way to save her would be to bicycle to her location. Would you be able to do it even if you weren't *in the "biking mood"*? If you can do the task to save her, you can also do it to *save yourself!*

For example, Jennifer is avoiding an important conversation with Kevin. Her apartment lease is about to expire. They had previously discussed moving in together by the time her lease would be up. Kevin knows this but has not mentioned it. Jennifer is afraid she will be putting too much pressure on him and she doesn't want to have an argument. Her waiting for Kevin to bring it up has not been helpful. She has been trying to push off the worry and stress without success.

In this case, Jennifer broke down facing the avoidance (*the conversation*) with Kevin into five parts. 1) Identifying and writing down how she is feeling and what she wants so she can communicate clearly. 2) Writing down how she believes he may respond. 3) Deciding how she would feel about the situation and what she would do. 4) Scheduling a "latest date" of when she will have this conversation. 5) Scheduling time to really have the conversation with Kevin.

This exposure to the issue caused a bit more stress initially, but after developing her "Then-What" plan to how he may respond, along with her "end date" of the conversation, she started feeling stronger and more in control. *(More about conversation skills in the next chapter)*. But wait!

Make a list of the tasks, chores, and activities you have been avoiding. These are tasks you know you should be tackling! This list is about YOU. It can be related to things *in* or *out* of your relationship.

List 5 Anti-Avoidance tasks that are important for you to be doing on a regular basis:

Anti-Avoidance Tasks:

1. _____
2. _____
3. _____
4. _____
5. _____

Pleasurable Activities

When you worry, get stressed, or feel down, do you do less pleasurable things? Many people do. People under chronic stress often say, "I used to really enjoy doing things. I used to have hobbies and see my friends, but I hardly do anything anymore. I haven't felt like it."

Perhaps you are the kind of person who has learned to put others' needs first. Does it get to the point where engaging in pleasurable activities seems selfish? Perhaps you feel as though you don't *deserve* to do anything pleasurable until __x__ happens.

Pleasurable activities can be anything that is (or used to be) fun! They can range from going out with friends, playing with your pet, reading, or engaging in a hobby, etc. The more you find your pleasurable balance, the more solid your mood will be. The more solid your mood, the more confident you will feel, and the easier it will be for you to move forward (however you decide to).

You can tap back into some of the things you used to enjoy. Or, you can explore a new area of interest that you've never pursued. Time? Even 15 minutes of reading, walking outside, or playing with your pet count! How about going to the movies or out for a ladies' night? It is your list. Remember, these activities *must not be time-consuming, expensive, or unrealistic* in fitting into your lifestyle.

List 5 Pleasurable tasks that you either used to enjoy or enjoy when you make the time:

Pleasurable Tasks:

1. _____
2. _____
3. _____
4. _____
5. _____

Authors' Note: *Accomplishment, Anti-Avoidant, & Pleasurable tasks can overlap with each other. You can see this in the chart below. Something you are avoiding can be pleasurable afterward. Scheduling pleasurable time can be an accomplishment, etc.*

The 15 Minute Rule

Our mind and body need time to adjust to things we don't *feel* like doing but would *benefit* from doing. This helps us get engaged in the task.

People who are successful at being balanced get started on tasks regardless of how they *feel*. People who tend to stay stuck avoid starting the tasks they don't *feel* like doing.

This is where the 15 minute rule comes in. It can be used with accomplishment, anti-avoidant, or pleasurable tasks. Any time you need a boost to get started because you've got a case of the "*I-don't-feel-like-its*," you can START engaging in the activity for 15 minutes. If after 15 minutes you still do not want to do it, then check it off your list as having done it! Small steps lead to big steps. You'll often find that you are (after 15 minutes) revved up and ready to dive in!

Increasing Your Balance - Putting It All Together

An ideal day is one in which you feel balanced. Jennifer reported feeling anxious and sad lately on the weekends. This was particularly the case when she was not seeing Kevin. Jennifer described the following as a typical weekend morning:

8am	9am	10am	11am	12pm
Sleep in	Check Facebook	Shower and get dressed	Run a few errands	Lunch at home

Now take a look at the example below. This shows Jennifer incorporating accomplishment, anti-avoidance, and pleasurable tasks in her morning.

8am	9am	10am	11am	12pm
Wake, do yoga	Breakfast while journaling her "then-whats" about her lease	Tidy up a bit	Shower and put on something fun to wear	Lunch out with girlfriend

Once Jennifer started incorporating all these tasks into her routine, she felt significantly less anxious and sad. Plus, the more she practiced the 15 minute rule to do things even when she didn't "feel like it," the more she became *more motivated* to do those things!

We have provided a day/evening chart below for you to fill in. Feel free to make copies of this chart or use your own calendar or planner. Start to track your daily activities. Incorporate at least one accomplishment, one anti-avoidance, and one pleasurable task daily for optimal mood enhancement!

8am	9am	10am	11am	12pm

1pm	2pm	3pm	4pm	5pm

6pm	7pm	8pm	9pm	10pm

It's important to remember to do these activities daily and *track your mood* as you go. This will help "uncover the mystery of your mood DNA." It will also help you work toward your balance and moving you onward!

Summary

In this chapter, you did a lot! First, we discussed the impact that the holding pattern can have on your mood (while keeping you stuck.) We also talked about the importance of grabbing onto *what is* in your control.

In order to rise above the holding pattern, you discovered your "mood DNA." You learned ways to improve your mood by incorporating daily healthy behaviors and activities. We have encouraged you to take control over how you spend your time. You increased your accomplishment, anti-avoidance, and pleasurable tasks in order to find your personal balance. We also discussed the power of the 15-minute rule. This allows you to start experimenting *now*, even *before* you "feel like it." The feelings will come later!

In the next chapter, we will teach you good communication techniques. These will assist you in communicating with your partner in an assertive (but also caring) manner. Healthy communication is the foundation for a solid relationship. It gives your relationship the best chance for success!

7

Putting Yourself Out There: communicating in order to be heard.

Talking the Talk

Everybody talks about how important "communication" is in a relationship. What does this really mean? The "talking heads" of morning radio, online bloggers, and T.V. show "therapists" all stress the importance of "communication." What is this magical concept, *really*? Why is it so important?

Webster's Dictionary defines communication as: "the act or process of using words, sounds, signs, or behaviors to express or exchange information or to express your ideas, thoughts, feelings, etc., to someone else." So, communication is *always going on in a* relationship. A distracted grunt from your partner when you ask him an important question is still, by definition, communication. It might not be the kind that you want or expect. So, when the "experts" tell couples "you are not communicating" and "you need to communicate more," what they really mean to say is that you ought to be communicating *better*. But how can people do this in or out of their relationships, especially if they were never taught?

Before we jump into sharpening up your communication style, let's revisit the relationship goals that you identified in Chapter 4. Please write them in below *(seriously)*.

Goal 1: _____

Goal 2: _____

Goal 3: _____

When you look back at your relationship goals, how many require good communication? From you or him? When you picture yourself as a good communicator, what do you see? The *basics* of a "good" communicator include knowing and sharing how you feel. It also means showing that you're listening! This is "active" listening. It involves showing attentiveness and reassuring that you understand what he is feeling. This sets him up to be calm and then able to listen to you.

When communication breaks down in your relationship, do you tend to blame each other? Do either of you get defensive? It can be a challenge to not get defensive or take things personally. When this happens, it's difficult for you or your partner to look at your own communication styles and how they can improve.

When a woman attends individual therapy, she might complain that she feels unhappy in her relationship. Her therapist might side with her, validate her perspective, and avoid challenging her point of view. This may help the woman to *feel* understood by her therapist, but it's not enough to help her in the long run. Her *own* communication style has to be assessed. This helps her take control over her part in the break down. She can keep her own communication on track and prevent the same problems from recurring.

In the next few sections, we will examine more closely the specific ways that *you* can improve the communication in your relationship. You can then perfect the ways that *you* can gain control, giving your relationship a better chance for success!

"Be Assertive, B – E – Assertive!"

The word assertive is defined as "confident in behavior or style." The definition may be simple, yet assertive communication takes practice to master. In particular, for those who have been raised in households in which the children were not encouraged to express their thoughts and feelings, in a family in which they had to be loud in order to be heard, or if their thoughts and feelings were *invalidated* by their caregivers, assertive communication can be particularly challenging.

Being assertive means communicating your thoughts or opinions in a *direct, clear, simple, and truthful manner. It is also done in a way that is sensitive and polite to the listener.* Assertion is communicating with a kind confidence. (When one speaks assertively, one has proper posture, steady tone of voice, and direct eye contact, with a neutral demeanor.)

Unfortunately, many people confuse *assertive* communication style with *aggressive* communication style. In addition, some therapists encourage their clients to be more "assertive" *while in fact teaching their clients that they are justified in behaving in ways that are actually "aggressive."* E.g., "*You should tell him how it is – and that you are not going to be a doormat!*" (*This is not assertiveness.*)

Many people think they are being assertive when they are being aggressive. For example, when a woman goes into a restaurant and glares at the waitress, asking in an agitated tone of voice whether or not they have freshly made, hot coffee, and upon receiving a stale cup of coffee, slams the cup back down on the saucer, causing some spillage, rolls her eyes, and grumbles, she is not behaving in a way that is assertive, *although she may think that she is.*

Additionally, being assertive is not about saying something to *control* how other people will respond, it is about *standing strong and confident no matter how they respond while doing so in a respectful manner.* This will be important to remember when you are communicating with your partner because as your emotions heighten, often your communication skills will suffer. You need not control how he communicates with you but you can successfully communicate your perspective to him, regardless of how he responds to you.

Authors' Note: *At this time, it's important for you to be the best you while also being goal-focused. So, no matter how he responds when you're communicating, you know you are doing your part to try and make it work!*

Speaking To Be Heard: Communication Techniques That Work!

People often say that they want to improve their communication skills with their partner but they really might not know *how* to do this. Improving communication is more than being able to speak and listen better. It's about building your assertive muscle. We start with an assertive template for you to learn and practice.

This first assertive-building technique is simple. It includes three parts: 1) describing the problem, 2) describing your feeling, and finally 3) stating what you would like. Situations arise in which you either feel like shutting down (avoiding) or lashing out. Working these steps are the most effective way to stay goal-focused with your partner without letting anger or defensiveness get in the way.

1 - Describing the problem

While describing the problem, it is important to use "I" statements like, *"It seems to me that we do not spend as much time together as we used to."* Notice there is no blaming or accusation in the description. It is your opinion. The problem is stated without an evaluation of the other person; it's just the facts!

2 - Describing my feeling

While describing the feeling, it has to be a FEELING (not a thought). Think of the emoticons on your cell phone ... the faces represent feelings (not thoughts). When you describe how you feel, go to the *soft* feelings. Soft feelings move your partner *toward* you when you are opening up. Going beneath any fiery anger, soft feelings keep things cool. They pull out your partner's nurturing side. They make for better listening, and prevent unnecessary defensiveness. Soft feelings are feelings like *hurt* or *fear* which is where most relationship problems lie. When discussing a problem from "hurt, fear, worry, or concern" any reasonable partner would want to help you to not feel that way. For example: "*I feel* hurt *because it seems to me like you do not notice this is bothering me. I feel* afraid *that you don't want me anymore."*

3 - What I would like

When stating what you would like it is important that you state it clearly. You can even offer up some problem solving ideas and see where you can be flexible. *"I would like to know if you want more time together and if so, what about scheduling a set date night?"*

Utilizing this template to springboard a talk with your partner will require a bit of practice. It *should* feel awkward initially because it's new! Still, doesn't it show *more* love to tolerate the awkwardness for the benefits of practicing good communication? There will be a bit of "editing" yourself initially – and that's okay. Think about it: Before you comment on a friend's Facebook post, don't you think about the comment before you post it? If you can think first for one of your Facebook friends, why not for him? It's important to remember to take a few deep breaths, slow down, and practice the 3 steps.

In order to highlight the use of this skill, we give the following example. While working with Linda, it came to light that she found it particularly hurtful when she needed Michael to be present for her during important times in her life. This happened most recently when her aunt passed away. Linda had been very close to her aunt and hoped that Michael would be able to attend the funeral with her. The funeral was only about one hour away. Michael reported that he was unable to attend the funeral due to work obligations.

When Michael told her he wouldn't be able to attend, Linda admitted to becoming very emotional and before hanging up on him she said, "I knew I would never be a true priority." Looking back on that day, she regrets how she reacted, particularly that she had hung up the phone on him out of anger after promising she would never do that. We worked with Linda on how she could communicate confidently to Michael using the 3-step technique we have just described. This is what Linda came up with:

3-Step Communication Technique

Linda:

Describe the Problem: *You are not coming.*

Describe the Soft Feelings: *I feel* hurt *you are not coming because my Aunt and I were close and I'm* afraid *you can never really be there for me.*

State What I Would Like: *I would like for you to really try your best to come for at least a part of the service. I also want some reassurance that you want to be here for me.*

Linda's response is in line with her goals of having open communication, being honest, and prioritizing each other in their relationship.

What have you avoided discussing with your partner? Think about something that you want to address. See if you can write it in the 3-steps below.

State the Problem *(Just the facts – no blame)*:

_____

Describe the Soft Feelings *(hurt or fear)*:

_____

State What I Would Like:

_____

_____

The OTHER WOMAN'S AFFAIR

Authors' Note: *We recommend practicing these 3-steps with small disagreements first - with anyone to get started. This way, there is no emotional investment. Practice with something like the Best Movie Ever. Or should the curtains be open or closed?*

Standing Confident No Matter What

What was it like for you to eloquently identify what to communicate to your partner? Did you like that style? Did it feel stronger or more confident? Knowing him, what are some of the things that you think he would say in response? Have you spent time thinking about how he would respond and do you try to avoid "difficult talks"? Do you think he will be supportive and nurturing or might he become defensive? If he is supportive, nurturing, and in a problem-solving mode, BINGO the 3-steps works! If he becomes defensive, that's okay too - there is more.

Now take a moment and brainstorm *three possible responses* that *he* may make about what you've shared. These responses are the things he says that lead you shut to shut down or blow up. Write them down, we will get to these responses very soon.

Many women have shared with us that they spent a lot of effort trying to be *his idea of perfect*. It was their way to be above any criticisms or to avoid letting him down. At this point, we want to be sure *you* are not avoiding important conversations. We want you to be able to stand strong while expressing your desires and putting yourself into the equation within the relationship. What would it be like to be kind yet also stand strong in this conversation?

Another assertiveness technique that is very effective and easy to remember is Christine Padesky's "assertive defense of the self." This technique consists of two parts: agreeing with what you can and then stating your position.

Agreeing With What You Can & Stating Your Position

Agreeing with a piece of what he says shows confidence. You are not outright disputing or becoming defensive. Remember, in this moment he is not trying to problem solve with you. He is criticizing your feelings or trying to convince you to feel another way. For practice, Linda identified 3 possible responses that Michael may make that would be difficult to handle:

1. *"Don't you think you are being unreasonable? I have an appointment!"*

2. *"You used to be able to do things alone."*

3. *"Do you not realize how busy I am?"*

Here, some of you might *shrink up* and doubt whether you are justified in wanting him to be there for you. Others may feel Michael's comments are selfish and get *escalated*. Linda experimented with this:

1. "Don't you think you are being unreasonable? I have an appointment!"

Linda: (1) *"Yes, I know you have an appointment."* (Agreeing).

Linda: (2) *"But no, I believe trying to problem-solve is reasonable."* (Stating position).

She repeated this template with the other possible responses:

2. *"You used to be able to do things alone."*

Linda: (1) *"Yes I did."* (Agreeing).

Linda: (2) *"And now we are together."* (Stating position).

3. *"Do you not realize how busy I am?"*

Linda: (1) *"I may not know the true extent of how busy you are."* (Agreeing).

Linda: (2) *"But nonetheless, I do know you are busy and I am trying to problem-solve."* (Stating position).

Let's go back to your 3-steps from the previous section. Write down some possible defensive or critical ways he may respond. See if you can come up with assertive defense statements for each (1) agreeing with what you can while (2) stating your position:

1. He may say: _____

I can agree with: _____

My position is: _____

2. He may say: _____

I can agree with: _____

My position is: _____

3. He may say: _____

I can agree with: _____

My position is: _____

It is important to rehearse these responses. If they arise, you will be able to stand strong and stay goal focused. He may not say these things, but you may see him think them. In these cases, you can use assertive defense responses in your head. You don't have to say them out loud to stand strong. Asserting helps you feel authentic. The way that you *want to be* in your relationship. No matter what happens, there will be *no regrets* on your part.

> **Recap**: This assertive defense exercise has 3 important purposes: 1) to help you be prepared to be confident however he responds, 2) to help you move toward your goals of having an intimate partnership in which both of your needs are being addressed, and 3) helping you gain mastery over your ability to regulate your mood and avoid shutting down or lashing out when unfairness or invalidation occurs with your partner.

Listening: With the Goal of Understanding

Yes! Assertive communication is important for closeness and trust. But how can he hear *you* if he thinks you're not listening to him? Good listening skills show your partner that you are attentive, engaged, and understand what he's saying. This puts him in a better mindset to listen.

A common pitfall in relationships occurs when messages between partners are misinterpreted. This is when one partner is *assuming* what their partner is trying to say. The following cliché example highlights this perfectly: A woman asks her boyfriend if he likes what she is wearing and he replies, "It's okay," and she responds with, "You think I look fat, don't you?" The woman is *attaching a negative meaning* to her boyfriend's statement. In order to prevent these kinds of communication problems, it is going to be important to improve your ability to *listen* to your partner to make sure that you clearly understand what he is saying. The first basic skill that we discuss is called Reflecting.

Reflecting – "I'm a Parrot with a Heart"

Reflecting is simple (*but not always easy*). It is summarizing what your partner has just said. This is done to clarify understanding. It portrays reassurance that "I understand" and it's done with a *neutral tone of voice.*

Your reflection is a statement, not a question *(Have your voice go down at the end of the reflection. Otherwise it sounds like a question.)* The simple act of your voice going *up* at the end of the statement is confusing. It makes your partner think that you *didn't* hear or understand what was said. This could cause misinterpretations and get things heated.

For example:

Linda <u>Questioning</u>, not really <u>Reflecting</u>:

Michael says to Linda: *"So, I will be able to pick you up right at the end of the funeral and we can go to the family dinner together."*
Linda: *"So you will be there at the end?"*
Michael: *"Yes, that's what I am saying."*
Linda: *"And you are going to come to the dinner?"*
Michael: *"Yes … that is what I am saying."*
Linda: *"So you will go?"*
Michael: *"YES, I will go!"*

The OTHER WOMAN'S AFFAIR

Reflecting with reassurance helps the speaker to elaborate and open up more about his feelings. It also prevents any negative assumptions or misunderstandings because you are confirming that you understand each other before jumping to any conclusions. It keeps the conversation focused and on track.

Linda Reflecting with Reassurance:

Michael says to Linda: *"So, I will be able to pick you up right at the end of the funeral and we can go to the family dinner together."*
Linda (*reflecting with reassurance*) *"You are coming at the end and then coming to dinner."*
Michael: *"Yes, I want you to know you're my priority."*
Linda: (*reflecting with reassurance*) *"You do want me to know that."*
Michael: *"I do. You know I love you."*
Linda: *"I love you too. We did a good job problem solving this."*
Michael: (*Now he's catching on*) *Yes, we did."*

By reflecting, Linda is able to get more information about how Michael feels. She is able to see that he is committed to prioritizing her. Also, that he is able to engage with problem-solving. Now she knows more about what is going on in Michael's mind.

Validation: Making a Deposit into the Relationship Bank

The second important listening skill that we discuss is called Validating. Most simply, this means to reassure that you understand the speaker's perspective and see his point of view. It is seeing the good intentions of what your partner is saying regardless of whether or not you agree with it. Common, basic forms of validation in conversation are phrases such as "Right," "That's true," or "Good point." It is better to be *specific* in what you are validating. He may say "*I have been so busy.*" And you may respond with a validation of, "*That is true, I know how busy you are!*"

If you *do not* fully agree with the speaker, that's okay. You can *seek out the parts with which you do agree.* You can *still* validate your partner even if you do not agree with him. When you validate someone's point of view, even when you disagree, you confirm to him that you *understand* his position while also backing up certain parts of his opinion.

Our earlier example of Linda coming up with an assertive response to Michael when she was validating him at the same time:

Linda: *"I may not know the true extent of how busy you are, but nonetheless I do know you are busy."*

Validation has huge benefits. It helps to calm tough talks, increase good listening, and helps you both stay close during disagreements. This makes for a discussion, diffusing a potential argument. You are essentially saying, "I see what you mean that_____; what you are saying about_____makes sense; and I understand how you can feel _____." Validation is the aspirin to your partner's defensiveness. When you *specifically* validate, you are being confident in your position. Your partner will be more likely to really listen to your needs and problem-solve if needed. You are finding common ground where you can both stand peacefully.

Summary

In this chapter, you have learned some very important communication techniques. Now you can practice "putting yourself out there" with confidence and skill. These tools can also help you *outside* of the relationship. Using these tools can help you face things you may have avoided while consumed with this relationship. It will also help you get in touch with your concerns, helping you to assert your needs and stand strong.

Experimenting with the 3-steps and assertive techniques will get your points across clearly with confidence. Practicing good listening and validation skills daily will feel empowering. It reaffirms to *you* that you are giving your best efforts! You will be goal-focused *regardless* of what happens with him.

Next, we'll work on keeping you "on track" by creating a timeline. Your time is precious and important!

STEP THREE

It's a Long-Run Game

8

Keeping You on Track – Seeing the Big Picture

Time Don't Give Me Time

Life goes by fast. If your partner can put a time frame on what would be considered "*too soon*" for you to be together exclusively, why can't he put a time frame on what would be "*too long*" to wait? If he could do that, you'd be able to decide whether you can accept his time frame. Perhaps he had one already and it passed with no changes in the relationship?

Suppose he was purchasing a car or house. Would he have to wait a year or two for the "*right*" car or the "*right*" house? If he cannot act on the good thing that is *the relationship you share,* what shall we surmise? His failure to act is not a mystery. It can be understood in one or more of the three categories below:

1) Desires vs. Goals

He has a *desire* to spend time with you. He *enjoys* the freedom and connection he feels when you are together. He may even *wish* the two of you could run away together. But desire, enjoyment, and wishes are not the same as *goals*. More time won't necessarily make a difference.

Putting the idea of "us" into a true goal would mean that he must make big choices. He would need to follow through. *Things would have to give.* In order to have a *goal* to start a life with you, he would have to mourn the fact that he could *not* "have it all."

2) Contradictory Values

We (the authors) both enjoy buffet-style meals because we like to be able to eat a variety of foods! But we *also* appreciate good *quality* food and service. Often, there is a contradiction between a buffet and fine food. Clean, fresh buffets with both high-quality foods *and* good service are hard to find. Therefore, we must accept the reality that we must sacrifice either quality or quantity. We can't always have it all while dining out – and in life in general!

Each of us wants certain things *more* than other things. This relates to what we *value*. Time does not necessarily make someone adopt a different value system. There's a rank-order that exists in our heads when it comes to ranking our values (whether we want to admit it or not.) What *he* values may be distinctively different than what *you* value.

He likely *strongly* values his sense of freedom with you as well as the connection and intimacy you share. Contradicting this, he likely also values being admired by his family, maintaining his financial status, and being seen as a "family man." You probably share many of the same values overall. The rank order may be different for the two of you – and it is certainly not personal.

3) Fear of Making the "Wrong Decision"

Fear of making the "wrong decision" leads to avoiding making a decision altogether! Time will *not* provide a crystal ball that will give him the certainty he wants. He will always just have 3 choices: 1) to make it work with you; 2) to remain with his wife; or 3) to ride this time period out until external forces (*you being fed up or his wife at her wit's end*) make the final choice *for* him.

He may be afraid of "history repeating itself." Perhaps he's worried about you both "falling out of love" in the future. Or, after being unhappy with his wife, he has a renewed sense of confidence in himself. He may be influenced by "settle" thinking such as, "Wow, this is great! What else is out there?"

He may also be fearful that he will not recoup his financial losses. Or, that his children will be forever damaged and never forgive him. Regardless, he believes he *must have* a guarantee that those "worst-case scenarios" *won't happen*. This belief comes from anxious thinking. Most realistically, he'd survive financially and the kids would eventually move on.

If he is "unable" to set a timeline or it has already passed, creating a timeline will be up to *you*. You're free to determine what sort of timeline would be considered too long. This choice is something that's in *your* control. It will keep you *goal-focused* and on track!

Your Time on the Line - Creating a Timeline

Your Limits

Limits. We all have them. When we were children, our caregivers may have either set too many limits with us or not enough. Sometimes we aren't sure if *we are allowed to set them*. Or sometimes we are *afraid to do so*. As adults though, if we do *not* set them, they will be *set for us*. Our future can be constructed by design or by default.

Although it may be difficult to believe, we've established that your love life is in your control. You may not be able to make him do what you believe is best for all. But, you can choose to hang in (or not) and set a limit.

What do YOU believe is a reasonable amount of time for you to keep hanging in? There is no right or wrong answer. We are looking for you to consider what's reasonable considering things take longer than expected. Perhaps it is past the time, but not yet past your limit?

This was the case for Jennifer. "When I first found out about Kevin being married, I told myself that I could give the relationship a solid six months. After that time, I would walk away if no concrete changes were made."

One year later, Jennifer realized that her initial timeline had expired. But, she hadn't yet reached her *limit*. She knew she could hold out for just a little bit longer. She also knew in her gut, though, that her limit would come very soon. However, the trouble with the word "soon," is that it is *vague*. The concept of "soon" could be tomorrow … or a year from now.

The following exercise entails creating a two-part timeline. First, we put a date on that vague idea of "soon." Time will slip away otherwise. Second, we break down the timeline even further. We add other relationship goals that you would like to accomplish.

We did this exercise with Jennifer. First, she circled her *absolute limit* of how long she was willing to wait for change. We asked Jennifer, "*What* needs to happen and by *when* does it need to happen for you to keep hanging on?" After some careful consideration, she decided, "I'll give him two months to file for divorce. If he doesn't do it by then, I will need to leave him."

Jennifer's Timeline (Part 1):

| 1 week | 1 month | 2 months | 3 months | 6 months | 1 year | 3 years |

To complete the second part of her timeline, Jennifer considered all her relationship goals. She started with the one furthest out in the future: getting married to Kevin. It's easier to start with further-out goals and then fill in the timeline backward. This is the most logical way to come up with realistic time-frames for each goal. Take a look at the second part of Jennifer's timeline below.

Jennifer's Timeline (Part 2):

In This Intimate Relationship, I Desire:

Being married to Kevin by this time:_____2 years from now_____

Sharing relationships with our families and friends by this time:___6 months from now___

Dating in an open/transparent way by this time:_____2 months from now_____

My limit for him filing for divorce by this time:_____2 months from now_____

My limit for him telling his wife it's over between them by this time:_1 month from now_

Communicating what I want by this time:___This weekend when I see him____

Now it's your turn to fill in both timelines. We have provided each one on separate pages. You can cut them out and post them as reminders. This will be helpful to you if you have been having difficulty setting limits.

For Part 1, circle (or write in) your *absolute limit*. For Part 2, fill in the sheet using realistic time frames that you can really stick to. Start by considering your most important relationship goal that is furthest out in the future. For example, is it being married or living in a domestic partnership? If you had to pick a date for this milestone, what would it be? When do you really want to be settled down comfortably with your partner? Start here, then move backwards to today. Are you having difficulty developing your timeline? Think about what you'd recommend to a friend going through a similar situation.

My Timeline (Part 1):

| 1 week | 1 month | 2 months | 3 months | 6 months | 1 year | 3 years |

My Timeline (Part 2):

> ***In This Intimate Relationship, I Desire:***
>
> **Being married/cohabitating with my partner by this time:**_____
>
> **Sharing relationships with our families and friends by this time:** _____
>
> **Dating in an open/transparent way by this time:** _____
>
> **My limit for him filing for divorce by this time:** _____
>
> **My limit for him telling his wife it's over between them by this time:** _____
>
> **Communicating what I want by this time:** _____

Remember To Be Realistic

Some of you may struggle with this exercise. Perhaps you want *all* of the above milestones to occur immediately. You might be saying to yourself, "I can't come up with different dates for these things because I want them all to happen right now."

It makes sense that you'd *desire immediate change* but how *realistic* would that be? You also might be concerned about how he will react to the idea of this timeline. You may wonder, "What is the point of this exercise?" But the point of it is that it's for you, not for him. You can space out the timelines for the above events in logical, realistic increments. They will represent milestones in the progression of your relationship.

To Tell or Not to Tell

Should you tell your partner about the timeline or keep it to yourself? We recommend telling him about your limits. This would be the equivalent of letting him "see your cards." And why shouldn't he? This gives him the information he needs to know to weigh all the factors. Not telling him would be playing a game. We advocate for you being straightforward and "being your best you" throughout this whole process.

Have you already communicated your timeline? Perhaps there is no need to re-hash it again. If he is unaware, though, telling him about it models the honesty and transparency you want in your relationship. Your timeline will lead him to truly assess his value system. It will assist in helping him further realize that something has to give.

Another benefit of communicating about the timeline is that his *reaction* will reveal important information. If he becomes defensive, you will be seeing a Red Flag unfold.

It's Not an Ultimatum, it's a Boundary

Suppose he becomes defensive and thinks you are giving him an ultimatum. This reaction from him might throw you off kilter. It can be easy to freeze up and become tongue-tied when he presents an argument that seems reasonable in the moment. Using your communication skills will help you respond back to him.

The fact is, it's not an ultimatum. It's a boundary that you are setting to care for yourself. It indicates when you have finally reached your limit. And you're the only person who can set that boundary with your best interests in mind.

Adding Your Personal Goals to the Timeline

Now we would like you to take your timeline and kick it up a notch. Remember, we promised you that we'd help you "reclaim your life"! Adding your personal goals to your timeline reminds you to invest in *you*. The relationship goals are important, but so are the personal ones. Adding these into your timeline reminds you where *you* fit into the bigger picture.

Jennifer realized that she's had an important personal goal for quite some time. She has always wanted to run her own business. Jennifer shared, "Ever since I was a kid, I knew I wanted to be my own boss. I really don't like working for the gym. I get paid a fraction of what I would make as a private personal trainer. I know I'm really good at what I do. I have a lot of ideas for how I could build my business. Whenever I go on Facebook, I see some of my friends who've become pretty successful over the years. One of them even has her own restaurant and she's doing really well. I get sort of jealous and I wonder why I haven't been doing the same thing for myself." (This had been one of the reasons that spending time on social media websites was causing Jennifer to feel anxious and depressed. We pointed this out in Chapter Six when she tracked her anxiety.) Jennifer knew that she would be able to start her business gradually while still working at the gym. She made a decision to get started on a business plan and marketing herself right away.

Below is Jennifer's more comprehensive timeline. This includes her relationship *and* personal goals marked at the times she'd like to accomplish them.

1 week	1 month	2 months	3 months	6 months	1 year	3 years
Starting today, Post Ad On Craigslist For Personal Training Services	Have one personal client by this time	Attend Fitness Conferences and Network		Have Website up and Running Build clientele		Fully Self Employed
Tell Kevin About my Timeline	Kevin to tell his wife	Kevin to File for Divorce		Kevin moves in with me		Married by now

Notice that Jennifer has two tracks: her own career and her relationship with Kevin. Also, notice that both tracks are not contingent upon one another. Regardless of what ends up happening on the Kevin track, Jennifer will be full-steam-ahead on her career track.

We encourage you to add your personal goals to your timeline as Jennifer did. Did you already start chipping away at them in Chapter Six? Additionally, have you noticed improvement in mood now that you've been doing accomplishment, anti-avoidance, and pleasurable activities?

Keeping focused on moving forward, write in things that you not only have to do in order to stick to your timeline in your relationship, but also what you have to do to *reclaim your life* regardless of the outcome with your partner. Pay extra attention to the *life goals* you may be avoiding. Also remember to make sure there is more pleasure in your life!

Summary

We have raised the stakes in this chapter. Time does not give you time. We outlined three of the possible reasons he may be holding back from moving forward in life with you at this crucial point. There are: desires versus goals; contradictory values; and fear of making the "wrong" decision. You have the choice to make a structured timeline, including both personal and relationship-oriented goals. We recommend communicating this timeline to your partner. "Soon" is a comforting concept to both of you. But, just as you learned in Chapter Six, one cannot wait until one "feels like" doing an action in order to take action. Taking action often needs to come first!

9

Facing Avoidance

Psst ... have you been avoiding our exercises so far? Remember, just like working out at the gym, the more you exercise, the easier it gets!

You've just set timelines marking your limits with a timeframe that's acceptable for you. We've also discussed focusing on your personal and relationship-oriented goals. We know this is an important relationship! Despite what you're learning so far in this book, it's natural that you might be avoiding putting our exercises into practice. Some of our exercises take a lot of hard work! But, putting them off might be messing with your ability to stand strong right now.

Avoidance and Motivation

Avoidance: we are all victims of it! Ninety nine percent of people do it when they are in an uncomfortable situation. The other 1% is simply waiting for the right time to admit that they're doing it!

Whether it's having difficult discussions with him using the tools we've provided or re-investing in time for you, avoidance may be getting in your way. Feelings of stress and anticipation may also be blocking you. It's an important step to first identify that you are anxious about the next move.

Anxiety and excitement are actually cousins. It's exciting to be able to take control over your life and move forward! But anxiety can be tempting you to keep things at the status quo. If you're struggling at this point, it will benefit you to do the following. 1. Accept the fact that you're afraid to have the important conversations with him and follow through on our exercises. 2. Accept the fact that things *do not* have to unfold with him the way you *wish* they would.

When you hold back from having difficult conversations with him or taking healthy steps toward moving forward, you end up strengthening the stuck-ness. *You end up practicing what you don't want to practice – more of the same!*

1) You strengthen the habit of *not speaking up* for yourself in a constructive manner.

2) You *practice avoidance* rather than truly connecting with your partner in a real and transparent way.

3) You *avoid developing the skills* you need to have the healthy relationship you desire.

4) You strongly *indoctrinate* yourself over and over again about the *awfulness* of *"upsetting the apple cart"* and the *awfulness* of the reality that *you may have to move on*.

I Avoid, Therefore I'm Safe – Philosophies of Avoidance

We all have philosophies that we live by. We have them because they help us (or at least they used to). During big transitions in our lives, in order to grow, we need to revise these principles by which we live. These principles *served us* during an earlier phase in our lives. Eventually, though, they run their course and *hold us back*.

Is there an old philosophy in play that is keeping you stuck? Let's look at two examples of Maria's "avoidance philosophy." We discovered this while uncovering her avoidance with telling Daniel about her timeline.

Maria's Avoidance Philosophy:

"If I avoid the discomfort of <u>sharing my timeline for him to leave her</u>, then <u>he can't get angry or pull away</u> and I will feel <u>connected</u>."

"Because if I don't <u>keep my timeline to myself</u>, then <u>he will pull away</u>, and I will feel <u>anxious</u>."

Here, Maria is avoiding for the purpose of preventing anger and frustration. She's making efforts to stay close to Daniel. With avoidance though, she can *only be so close*. Further procrastination will only take her further away from her goals.

We also helped Jennifer uncover two examples of her own "avoidance philosophy."

Jennifer's Avoidance Philosophy:

"If I avoid the discomfort of <u>talking about my desire to start a family</u>, then

<u>I'll find the "right time"</u> and I will feel <u>relieved</u>."

"Because if I don't <u>wait for the right time</u>, then <u>it will go horribly and I will lose out</u>, and I will feel <u>anxious</u>."

Here, Jennifer is stuck. She has good intentions: waiting for the right time to take action because she wants it to go well. But what if the "right time" never comes? The stars might never align perfectly. Eventually, you will have to face the discomfort of following through.

What's behind *your* avoidance? Let's get down to the heart of how avoidance might be getting in your way. Fill in the blanks below:

My Avoidance Philosophy:

If I avoid the discomfort of _____ (the task I've been avoiding), then _____ (the unwanted event) will not happen, and I will feel _____ (insert the relieved feeling).

Because,

If I DON'T avoid _____ (the task I've been avoiding), then _____ (the feared event) will happen, and I will feel _____ (insert the dreaded feeling).

Safety Behaviors

In order to mitigate our anxiety, we tend to engage in things called "safety behaviors." *The act of avoiding itself is done by doing safety behaviors.* Safety behaviors are also things we believe we must do in order to protect ourselves from something bad happening. At their extreme, they can also look like "good-luck rituals" that need to be done in order to prevent a bad outcome. For example, saying a prayer before taking off in an airplane in order to prevent a plane crash.

You might be engaging in safety behaviors to make the relationship "work out." In actuality, though, these behaviors help you *avoid addressing the things that really matter to you.* Below is a list of common safety behaviors, done with the good intention of avoiding conflict:

1. Prepping yourself to look your best before you see him. For example, getting your nails done, shopping for new outfits, doing your hair and make-up the way he likes, etc.

2. Acting "as-if" you are always "fine" when you are with him. You do this even when you feel upset beneath the surface.

3. Frequent drinking alcohol or using recreational drugs in order to cope with your emotions.

4. Over-using anti-anxiety medication or sleep aids to relax, block out your anxious thoughts, and control your emotions.

5. Becoming enmeshed with a friend who is going through a crisis. This helps you focus on her problems rather than your own.

6. Spending *a great deal* of time at the gym or with friends to avoid being alone with your thoughts.

Have you been avoiding addressing any of the following with your partner?

-He still has not moved out of his home.

-He still has not told his wife that their relationship is *really* over.

-He still has not filed for divorce.

Overcoming Avoidance

The good intention here is that you want to be emotionally safe. But at the same time, you may be keeping the status quo! If you are okay with the status quo, then all is well and good. You will certainly survive it while even having joy along the way.

However, if you want to design a life geared toward your *desires*, you'll need a *philosophical upgrade*. We'll have to construct *new* true and healthy beliefs. These will help you push through with your goals and timeline. Before we construct new beliefs, let's armor up!

Recycling Your Strengths

What is something that you do daily because you really enjoy doing it? Is it having your morning cup of coffee, taking your dog for a walk, or texting with your best friend? Think of the *personal strengths* you have that keep you *committed* to these daily tasks.

What are the qualities about yourself that keep you strong in certain areas of your life? Has your ambitious nature helped you succeed in the workplace? Has your curious intellect helped you be a high-achieving scholar? Is your kind-hearted demeanor what attracts many friends to your side?

The strengths you have in certain aspects of your life can benefit you in the areas in which you struggle! If you're disciplined in certain things, such as caring for your pet, you can also be disciplined in caring for yourself! If you're able to nurture others *regardless of how you feel* because you're *committed* to it, then you're also capable of practicing a commitment to *nurturing yourself*. Strengths *can carry over* and benefit you in bigger ways than they do now. You can use those strengths to overcome your avoidance!

New "Push-Through" Beliefs

You Have To See It To Feel It: An Exercise

Picture one of the areas in your relationship that you're avoiding dealing with even though it's in your timeline. This could be anything related to an important discussion you want to have with him. Now, imagine, like watching yourself in a movie, picture yourself actually facing your avoidance. Focus in on this picture and imagine yourself doing what you've been avoiding *with confidence*. If you're having difficulty seeing yourself doing this, think of a friend, an actress, or a strong character you admire who is confident and could do it! See if you can borrow those qualities and create that image. What do you see? How do you feel? Does it remind you of a time when you were confident and brave?

While conjuring up those images, certain beliefs might have still been getting in your way. If so, that's to be expected. Remember what you did in Chapter Five? You came up with *new beliefs* to replace the *old ones* that kept you stuck.

Again, focus on the image of yourself confidently "pushing through." When you have that strong image, write in the new "push-through belief" below:

If I push through and _____, then _____, and I will
                    (uncomfortable action)   (likely result)

feel _____.
     (positive emotion)

If I do not _____, then _____, and I will feel
             (uncomfortable action)   (likely result)

_____.
(negative emotion)

Now, if you believed this healthier, more helpful rule, what would you actually be doing *instead of avoiding? How would you do it?*

Maria developed a new push-through belief. See below.

Maria's New Push-Through Belief:

If I push through and <u>share with him my timeline</u>, then <u>I can address what I need, and see if he</u>
             (uncomfortable action)   (likely result)

<u>can agree</u>, and I will <u>feel confident.</u>
                            (positive emotion)

If I <u>don't share with him my timeline</u>, then <u>I cannot address my needs and</u>
             (uncomfortable action)   (likely result)

<u>I will feel more anxious.</u>
     (negative emotion).

Maria believed her new push-through belief was logically true and healthy. She could see how strongly believing this would empower her. It would help her talk to Daniel openly and directly about what she wants! But ... she didn't really believe that talking to him would yield positive results. Therefore, Maria tested out this new belief, which will soon follow below.

Experimenting With Your New Belief

Experiments are the best way to test things out, especially new beliefs! Now, when you test out your new belief, you have to be careful. You *cannot* have a goal of "making him respond the way you want him to." You cannot have goals to change *other people's* behaviors. This type of goal will only bring you back to avoiding again! Unfortunately, you do not get any guarantees! Waiting for a guaranteed response will bring you back to the stuck-zone. Here, the appropriate goal would be: "staying resilient and confident *regardless* of his response." *Here, it is not about the outcome. It's about being brave and making important choices about the type of relationship you want (and don't want)!*

Testing It Out & Risk-Taking

The "aspirin" for anxiety is "exposure"! Exposure is exactly what it sounds like. You start by first identifying specifically *what* you are avoiding. Then, you test out your new push-through belief to see if the situation was as anxiety-provoking as you had imagined!

You can even start by telling a friend what you have been avoiding and why. This way, you identify your fear, accept it, and take steps toward dealing with it. Pushing through the avoidance builds confidence and growth.

Unfortunately, confidence and growth don't come first! They develop through the "reps" of pushing through and *continuing to do what is uncomfortable*. Take fear of flying, for example. The "cure" is to literally take several flights while testing out a healthier belief system. Eventually, the confidence builds up until the fear can be handled like a champ!

Exposure at this point means *following through on your limits despite* any discomfort you feel. A good exposure is one in which you are willing to trade *short-term stress* for the *"bigger-picture" goal*. The bigger-picture goal would be *having the kind of relationship you desire*! Like a wave, the discomfort of facing your fears will come to a crest and eventually wash out!

Maria designed an experiment to test out her new push-through belief.

Maria's Experiment:

>The belief Maria tested out: *If I push through and share my timeline with him, then I can address what I need, and see if he can agree, and I will feel confident. If I don't share with him my timeline, then I cannot address my needs, and I will feel more anxious.*
>
>What Maria planned to do: *Have a conversation about my timeline with confidence.*
>
>What Maria believed was likely to happen: *He will try to avoid the discussion or make excuses.*
>
>How Maria planned to cope with it: *It would be difficult, but I'd survive it, and I'd have more information that tells me about his readiness.*

Now it's your turn to design an experiment to test out your new push-through belief.

Your Experiment:

>The belief I am testing out:
>
>_____
>(insert new belief here)
>
>What I plan to do:

(insert the strategy here)

What I believe is likely to happen:

_____

How will I likely cope with it:

_____

Forcing yourself to test out your push-through beliefs and assert your limits helps you reclaim control over what you want. It reinforces such ideas as, *"I deserve to have the relationship I desire!" "I am worth his making difficult choices." "I will be in a healthy relationship with or without him if need be!" "I can stand strong and follow through on what I believe is right for me!"*

It won't be perfect and backslides will happen. It's important that you work your *strengths* like a muscle. Continue to conjure up *confident images* while going over your new push-through beliefs. You're taking healthy risks for the relationship you desire!

Assessing the results:

What actually happened?

_____

How strongly did I believe my new philosophy?

_____

How did I actually cope?

_____

Still Struggling With Avoidance?

We've been offering tips and tools to help you push through on the road for the life you desire. Of course, you don't have to do any of it! You will still have an interesting life even if you avoid taking control. You can simply react to whatever happens and that would be okay!

However, you will have a more *enriched* life if you plan for the things you desire and take steps to carry out the plan. We don't think you'll regret tolerating the discomfort of some of the action required.

Helpful Reminders:

The Progress Thermometer

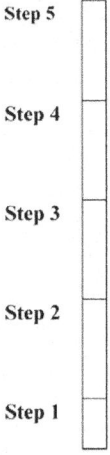

Imagine this thermometer "heating up" as you make progress on your goals to move forward. You can post this thermometer on your bathroom mirror, refrigerator, or even on a post-it note on your dashboard. Filling it in will keep your eye on "moving up" as you hit your goals.

The "Real" Big Picture

Another reminder is to look at a "big picture" on a regular basis. You can download one on your computer and phone. Every day, you can see this "big picture" and not lose sight of what you really want! Variations of this can be wedding or baby photos (if you want to have a family with a partner), or any image that would be motivating or inspiring to you.

Cyber-Stalk Yourself

Set up free email alerts from sites like Google. Use an online calendar to harass yourself with email reminders of the "importance of pushing through." Send yourself brief emails entitled "Why It's Worth It!" You can set these reminders daily or a few times per week so you won't lose sight of your goals during the week.

Grandmother's Rule

Peas before pudding! Schedule your pleasures *after* you have the difficult discussions with him and *after* you follow through on the limit-setting you may be avoiding. For example, put the important conversations before time out with your friends, going to a movie, or enjoying a sweet treat. Have the difficult task come first and then use the pleasurable as the reward!

"What's Worse?" – Making a Side Bet!

You can make a special side-bet with yourself. For example, you make a contract that states that you *must* push through by setting a limit in the relationship or else you *must* do another task that you are avoiding, such as going on a strict diet, organizing your taxes, or doing something related to your other personal goals. Every day that you *avoid* moving toward your relationship goal, you must engage in the alternative anti-avoidance activity!

Reward Your Enemy

Sometimes self-imposed consequences don't work and you have to be creative to get motivated! One of the authors has worked with a client who said, "In order to motivate myself, I will burn 100 dollars. This week, if I don't do my homework of having that conversation I know I need to have with my partner, I will burn 100 dollars!" One would think this incentive would be strong enough to help push through the discomfort. Plus, this particular person was on the frugal side! But, the incentive wasn't enough and that client burned the money right in the therapy office!

What usually creates motivation *in lieu of wasting money* is donating to an enemy. Are you Jewish? Donate to a Nazi organization if you don't follow through! Are you a Democrat? Donate to the Republican Party! (*You see where we're going with this?*) How many donations would you have to make to an enemy until you finally say, *"Okay, let's do this!"*

Use Confederates

If you cannot hold yourself accountable to what is best for you, contract out! Using confederates means enlisting the help of your friends and family. Tell them about the next step you will be facing. You will have their approval when you complete your next step! You will also get their disapproval if you do *not* complete your next step. This will certainly up the ante! You can also get your friends or family to *impose consequences* if you *don't* follow through with your next step by "X" time, and grant rewards if you do!

Put The Avoidance On Trial (In a Psychological Court of Law)

Are any of the following thoughts relevant for you? The "closing argument" is the logical argument *against* the thought. Put the "thought" on one side of a flash card and the "closing argument" on the other.

Thought: *If I wait until I get extremely fed up, it will be easier to assert my limit.*

The Closing Argument: *If I wait until I'm fed up, my anger won't let me communicate at my best. Being "fed up" doesn't* make me *face the issue. I could push through in many conditions, not just when I am fed up.*

Thought: *I don't know what I'm going to do if it doesn't work out, so there's no harm in waiting.*

Closing argument: *I actually do know what I'm going to do. If the relationship doesn't work out, I will mourn ... and then I will move on! It's not that I don't know what to do. I have moved on before. If I am truly unsure of what or how to do it, I can go back and complete the exercises in this book. If I don't know what I'm going to do, I better start figuring it out now. Life is too short to wait for courage. The courage will come later.*

Thought: *If I'm not following through on my limit, it must not be that important.*

Closing argument: *If it's not that important, I should just get it over with then! Whatever it is, it's an important part of my goal to move forward with my life. I could take a more passive route and still have some happiness, but I only live once! I deserve more!*

Thought: *The world won't come to an end if I wait longer.*

Closing Argument: *Yes, the world won't come to an end. But that doesn't mean this is not important for me to do! Should I only do things that would prevent the world from coming to an end? No. I am not a superhero crime fighter, just a human being trying to have happiness in my life!*

Summary

We really expounded on avoidance in this chapter, didn't we? We examined safety behaviors and why you might have been avoiding putting our exercises into practice. We also helped you identify your "avoidance philosophy" that's been holding you back. You came up with newer, healthier "push-through" beliefs to combat the old ones. We encouraged you to use other strategies to help you along even further. Enlisting the help of friends or "rewarding an enemy" were some examples. In the next chapter, we help you maintain your focus so you can continue "being your best you!" We know you've been working hard to do your best in this relationship.

10

Maintaining Your Focus: Being your best "you" without letting stress sabotage the relationship.

Has your deadline date passed yet? If not, you now have the opportunity to make your best efforts prior to the deadline! If the deadline has passed and you're not quite ready to follow through, consider: what more information do you need? There may be some possible stuck-points. For example, he may be moving too slowly, not filing for separation/divorce, etc. Do you feel like you've invested so much that you can't walk away?

Checklist For What You SHOULD Be Doing:

Examining the Situation

Is he Mr. Ready yet? You're asserting, setting time-limits, and having goals to design your next chapter in life. You've been working hard! How has he been responding?

It's helpful at this point to avoid making assumptions (positive or negative). Instead, focus on *facts*, his *behavior*, and what *you* can do. Remember that it's quite possible that he's coming from a place of good intentions. Nonetheless, it's important to examine the facts of what is *actually happening now. Have enough concrete steps occurred that you can verify or see?*

Accepting the Value Difference

A value difference just highlights the reality that the situation isn't perfect. There are different factors at stake for both of you. You can accept the value difference *without making it personal.* This means that you accept the differences in both of your scales of importance/priorities.

Accepting the value difference helps you stay focused as to whether this relationship is still working. It's not about "trying to win" his love. You likely have it already. It just may not be *enough* for the relationship to move past this point. The presence of love (for him) does not necessarily mean that things have to turn out the way you hope they will. Of course, it would be nice if they did.

Focus on the Double-Sided Traits

Don't block anything out in order to better cope with the situation. Is the current state of the relationship making you *only* focus on the *positive* aspects of his character (convincing you to wait for him regardless of the facts)? You should *also* be focusing *equally* on the side of him that is hurtful to you and contributing to the stuck-ness in your life. This is the reality. He is not just one-sided; he is a culmination of both sides.

Set "Balanced" Time Aside

Make sure to schedule time for stress-reducing rituals so you can both relax together. During these times, put relationship talk on a holiday. (He would like that too, right?) Engage in activities during which you can connect and nurture each other. But *also* make sure that you both schedule time to discuss the status of the relationship.

This includes looking at how things may be progressing (or not) and how you are both coping.

Set aside at least 15 minutes once a week to discuss the relationship. This will help keep you focused and stay on track with your plans. It will also help you avoid over-focusing on the problems in the relationship. Additionally, he'll be less likely to avoid spending time with you for fear that "issues" might get continually brought up. A minimum of 15 minutes per week of discussing the relationship communicates to one another, *"I take your concerns seriously and I am working on these things with you."*

Separate the Relationship from the Problem

The relationship itself has been good. You both get along and feel good with each other. You connect. The relationship is *not* the problem. *The problem is that the current environment is not healthy enough to sustain the relationship in its current state.* Like a beautiful floral bouquet in a vase, the life of the bouquet is time-limited. The flowers in their present state cannot survive their current environment.

There needs to be a change of environment or situation for the relationship. Otherwise, it will decompose. The reality is that the current intensity of the relationship cannot last without a cost. You likely are not the type of person who could put your feelings and desires in a box; (this is very hard to do). The only ways to keep your feelings in a box are ways that eventually hurt you. For example, using unhealthy distractions such as drugs, alcohol, shopping, etc. keep the box sealed, but at the expense of your health.

Get Closer To YOU

If you've been working the tools in this book and taking the recommendations, you've been working for a healthy outcome regardless of what happens in this relationship. Until he steps up or you're ready to let go, it's important to readjust your lens and focus more on *you*.

Many people have told us it feels "selfish" to do this. It might feel this way initially. But we want to remind you that self-*interest* is never *selfishness*! It's simply you focusing on what's *in* your control and accepting what's *not*. It's you focusing on improving things regardless of the outcome. If you really think about it, it's something that can never be regretted!

Checklist For What You Should NOT Be Doing:

It's too late in the game to engage in the following behaviors.

Expecting Him to Change

His value system, in theory, may not be the one he's expressed to you. His current choices and behaviors reflect his current values. This is who he is. If you see him as "stock" that may mature with time, you're playing too risky of a game!

If he hasn't changed yet, how long until he does? Would it take six months? Twelve months? Will the longer you wait make it more "worth" the wait or does it simply mean it's much riskier of a move? In our work, we often find that the best predictor of the future is looking at the past. It's not that people cannot change. But, if they *work hard to change and get real help,* it reduces the overall calculated risk.

Complaining/Guilt Tripping

At this point, he knows what he needs to do to share a life with you. Complaints will only breed resentment and more of the same behavior from him. How can you channel your complaints toward addressing your goals and timeline? Complaints or guilt tripping may be revealing *neediness* for him to do what you'd like instead of *simply a desire* for him to do so. Focusing on him changing more than focusing upon yourself does not let you take responsibility for your happiness. Your joy *is* in your control. Complaining has been shown to only deepen one's level of frustration while impairing one's ability to problem solve.

He likely already feels stress and frustration about the situation. Complaining and guilt-tripping make matters worse. The more emotional you get, the more he may see you as stuck and *giving up your control to him*. This will breed more frustration and nothing different will happen. You both may be creating the reality that you are "waiting" for him.

Questioning, Lecturing & Advice

"Why is it taking so long? Why haven't you filed yet? Why don't they know about us?" Have you caught the theme of these questions? These questions imply, "You are *not* handling this as you *should*!"

"Why" questions, lecturing, and unsolicited advice are rarely taken kindly by your partner and will lead you both to more frustration. What he is experiencing is an emotional issue. It's a safe bet that he knows all these gems of advice that you give him. He was savvy enough to know how to get and maintain your relationship! He likely knows what he *should* do now to move forward with you!

The more you question and lecture, the more he will want to *avoid dealing* with the situation. Questions at this point are like a broken record that will only lead to more of the same. Is it safe to say he knows how you feel at this point? Giving advice is a minor form of begging, "Please do the right thing!"

Constructive & Unconstructive Venting

Talking about the relationship status with family or friends can be helpful. The support of loved ones is definitely crucial. But it's important to keep in mind *how* you discuss the relationship. For example, discussing your plan, your limits, and how you are coping are all constructive ways of venting.

Focusing on the unfairness and how you feel stuck or trapped distracts you from your plan and accepting reality. This is unconstructive because it keeps you from problem solving and following through on a plan. Unconstructive venting leads to more emotional upset and eventual anger and resentment.

Sarcasm and Judging

When you are sarcastic or judgmental with him you are both still connected! However, this type of connection is an unhealthy one. It gives him the impression that *he is in control*, not you.

Beneath the sarcasm and judging lies your hurt and fear that he doesn't value the relationship as you do. It also represents your fear that the relationship will not succeed. If you are going to share your thoughts, why not take the higher road by discussing your hurt and fear?

Speaking directly from the hurt and fear helps you exist in reality and accept his process. It also provides him one more opportunity to validate your feelings. He can then decide what changes, if any, he wants to make. Speaking in a sarcastic or judgmental manner will lead him to feel resentful.

Avoiding

If you don't take any action now, when will change occur? In one month? Three months? One year from now? When you avoid, you seek *safety and security* instead of *moving toward your goals. Is your avoidance really keeping you safe or just keeping you in a holding pattern?*

If you're avoiding moving forward in your relationship, when will the time come if not now? More avoidance is taking up your time and giving it over to him. *Avoidance does not buy him time. It gives it to him for free.*

Thinking Things But Not Saying Them

At this point, you should be speaking your mind openly. There's nothing to hide. Sure, "editing" what you say is helpful so you can be heard and get your point across. But holding back is not accomplishing anything. Being a "good girl" doesn't put you in a collaborative partnership. It's neither going to help you be heard or guarantee anything to happen. Keeping things to yourself can make your concerns get over-looked. It can also lead you to be more passive when trying to attain your goals.

Opening up will eliminate the "I should have said _____" moments. There can be no regrets! Moreover, if you end up reaching your limit and moving on, he may say you should have told him earlier. This could lead you to doubt and regret later decisions. Speaking up now (if you still haven't) will create a chance to problem-solve together. Are you holding in your thoughts and feelings from him? Communicating them and then letting go will relieve your excess stress.

Being Your Own Worst Frenemy

In some ways, the areas you might be focusing on can be your "worst enemy" and not your "best friend." For example, you might have been focusing on how "free" you feel in this relationship. But you've been living with ambiguity as if you're in a movie with no real ending! Yes, you never really had anyone to "answer to" yet you were never completely alone. However, the very parts of the relationship that make you *think* you're free *keep you bound*. You're now in a situation in which you cannot, solely, control the outcome unless you make a *conscious choice to do so*.

Now It's Time To Re-focus And Re-frame!

Are you focusing on whether you will "find anyone else"?

This is a common yet unhelpful focus. Remember when you were coming out of your last relationship? Did you have the same worry at the time? And did you "find someone else"? You did! When was the last time you were *really alone* while you were *actively trying to be in a relationship*? Besides, haven't you *already felt alone* at times during this relationship?

Re-focus on the fact that you *can* and *do* connect with others. You've had these fears before and they were unsubstantiated.

There's no reason to think that the *last* man the forces of nature brought to you is a married one. Re-focus on what *you* are looking for and what *you* want. Re-focus on where it is likely that you would be able to find those things. Waiting for forces to *come to you* may likely bring you a Mr. Charming before a Mr. Ready. *Mr. Ready often needs you to be looking for him as well!*

Are you focusing on the concept of "settling"?

You might believe that you'll never have a better relationship. Or, you might question whether you *deserve* to have more. Perhaps your experience is that you've had "bad luck" in relationships before, so why should anything change, and why should you expect any different?

Re-focusing on *what you want* will organize you in such a way that you'll be able to go after it. Where do you find a single Mr. Ready? Mr. Ready is in places where other singles are looking for people. Places such as singles events, spiritual groups for singles, and social media sites for singles are all good places to look.

Are you focusing on the "bottom of the barrel" as representing your dating pool?

Do you see your partner through rose-colored glasses? If so, you could be tricked into thinking that he's the "best" you can get and if you choose someone else, you'd be "settling." What if you are settling now? We know your partner has great qualities and we've made this assertion from the start. However, according to U.S. census data, he's not the only man out there with wonderful qualities! There are actually over 51 million adult men who are single in the US alone.

Re-focus on gathering data that others are out there with good qualities. For example, look up singles events and see the men who are involved. You can also sign up on a reputable dating website for people really looking for a long-term partner. Men are everywhere. Much like the female contestants on "The Bachelor," you've been focusing for too long on *one option*.

Are you focusing on society's expectations of where you should be in your life?

Are you preoccupied with your biological clock? Are your close friends appearing "happily married"? Do they have children? Do you believe that you may as well "see this whole thing out" because it would be too late to find someone else with whom to start a family? Do you think that you "should" have been at a certain place in your life by now and you want to force that "should" to happen, like trying to fit a square peg into a round hole?

Re-focus on what is right for you now, but also flash-forward a year from now and see if what you are doing is getting you on track. If not, refocus back to what needs to be done, as we discussed in Chapters Four and Eight. Revisit your goals and your timeline. This way, you can be sure you are living your life and not anyone else's.

Are you focusing on not having "failed"?

Many women with whom we speak believe, "If this relationship fails, then I have failed. I cannot stand to be seen as a loser by my friends and family. I am in too deep, this has to work. I can't fail." The concept of failure is so harsh and unnecessarily brutal! Do you consider President Lincoln a failure? After all, he lost four public office elections before he became President. In relationships, you can never "fail," unless you completely and utterly refuse to learn from the experience. So long as you can learn in life, there is no failure!

Re-focus on the successes that you've had striving to be the best you (keeping in mind you are a fallible human) that you can be. As you continue to be your best you, you can let go of regrets. Re-focusing on the fact that you took the risk and went for it shows that it was a worthy pursuit. Anything worth pursuing is worth failing at. The relationship may run its course but that doesn't mean YOU are a failure. Choose to focus on learning from the experience.

Summary

In this chapter, we discussed getting you focused with a fine-toothed comb! We've refined both what you should focus on and what you should not focus on. We also got you to reframe some of the worries that may still be holding you back. In the next chapter, examine how all your hard work has been paying off so far. Now you can assess how he's been responding to the changes you've been making.

11

Knowing When to Hold 'Em: Identifying promising signs that indicate relationship success.

How's It Going So Far?

You've been working to make some changes in the way you approach your relationship: setting goals, managing your anxiety, and improving your communication skills (just to name a few things). How has he been responding? Same-old or something new? Besides what he is verbally *saying* about these changes, how is he behaving? Have your efforts been met with enthusiasm and support or with resistance and avoidance?

These are important facts to collect and to *honestly* consider. If your partner has really made concrete, significant changes *that you can see*, those would be the best of all the promising signs. However, we are aware that the changes he makes might be more subtle and you might need to use your discerning abilities. While working our program, this chapter helps you determine whether he is showing you promising signs.

The Healthy Track

We start first by doing a quick over-view about healthy relationships. Many people, both men and women alike, with whom we've worked over the years, have told us they really didn't know what a "healthy" relationship looked like.

A partner who truly loves, respects, and cares about you will desire to be committed. He wouldn't want to continue engaging in deceptive practices with you and his family. As you know, though, relationships are complicated. People get married for a variety of reasons with the *best of intentions for things to work*. When the relationship ends, it can be a struggle to go through the acceptance and letting-go process, even when feelings of being *"in love" are gone*. When couples do not grow together, the relationship tends to run its course. You and your partner may feel as though you are "perfect together," but is your relationship on a healthy track?

Nearly everyone wants to have "the best" relationship. The pursuit of the perfect partner is all around us: online, in pop culture, movies, and TV shows. Most people are somehow involved, or trying to be involved, in a romantic relationship. Many people place a lot of their own life happiness on whether or not they are with the *"right partner."*

If achieving this ideal is difficult enough, how do you do it when the relationship starts from a place of deceit? How do you know if your relationship can actually reap the benefits of your "hanging in there"? Typically, the happiest of romantic relationships are based upon the establishment of a *deep friendship*. Although opposites may attract initially, couples with a deep friendship and common values experience the most long-term relational satisfaction.

There are some misconceptions about the factors that cause a relationship to run its course. Some common beliefs include:

relationships don't work between people with *different personalities* and *frequent arguing* destroys a relationship. These myths have been debunked. It's possible to have a successful relationship with someone whose personality is different from yours. The key to success is finding a way to manage the differences in ways that work for both of you. In addition, frequent arguing doesn't have to lead to relationship suicide. It is *how* you and your partner argue that makes the difference.

We're about to cover the most promising signs that indicate when to "hold 'em." These are based off our research, clients' experiences, and *all the hard work you've been putting in so far*. Of course, this information does not apply to *every* situation. It cannot *predict* his behavior with 100% certainty. We *do* encourage you to use these signs to examine your relationship both *as it stands now* and the way you interact with your partner in general.

Six Promising Signs

Promising Sign #1: Taking *active* steps to separate (emotionally/physically) from his wife. He not only has concrete plans to move on, he is openly discussing them with you. Taking visible steps toward those plans, he knows how important this is for you. For example, he has met with a divorce mediator or attorney to discuss his options. He is protecting his assets while attempting to have transparency with you. This may mean opening his phone or email accounts to you to assist you in building your trust during this vulnerable time.

He has moved out of their master bedroom and into a guest room, onto the couch, or has moved out altogether. (*Many men say they are in another room or on the couch and often this is not the case!*) He does NOT describe his wife as a "best friend." (*Many men will stay with their wives ultimately for the friendship*). If this "best friendship" exists, he's likely still in the same bedroom with her because he's comfortable and doesn't want to upset the applecart at home.

Daily family routines are limited to dealing with the pets or children, such as coordinating getting them to school or attending to their extra-curricular activities (in most instances, the kids' not the pets'!) He does not spend time with his wife in *any* sort of intimate way, whether *physical or emotional.* They emotionally live two separate lives, as roommates, and this distinction is *clear* to the *both of them.* When problems arise between he and his wife, you are seeing fewer signs of him being shocked, hurt or angered by her behavior and more of an acceptance of who she is and an eagerness to move on.

Promising Sign #2: You wouldn't be a surprise! Maybe she does not know about you with certainty but his wife would not be surprised that you exist. He may be keeping you on the "D.L." because he is trying to keep a low profile during this transition. His friends and family may know there are problems in his marriage and they would *not* be surprised by a divorce. *(Men who value the way their marriage "looks" on the outside also tend to value the "image of the family" and "outside perception" over being transparent.)* If some of his colleagues know about your "friendship" and you are included in some parties or work functions, then of course that is even better!

Promising Sign #3: He has a good friend and you know him. In general, having a close male friend indicates that he strives for balance. His friendship may be a sign that he is capable of good reciprocity in his close relationships. Moreover, when he discusses his friend, he speaks highly of him.

His friend preferably has a good, healthy relationship with his own partner as well. He does not paint this friend as a "player" and the friend does not engage in affairs himself. Perhaps his friend is even a healthy role-model who is helping him at this time. It is an even better sign if this friend not only knows about you but your partner is also comfortable with total transparency in his relationship with you and him.

Promising Sign #4: You are in his future plans. At this point, he should know how important this is to you, and it's important to him as well. He discusses his future plans specifically with you – not in the form of a dream that would be nice, but as plans that will occur. When he plans ahead for life "post separation/divorce," he asks you for your opinions and your preferences. There can be discussions of whether it's better to initially live apart or together during the filing of divorce through when it's finalized. He's interested to share with you his ideas of daily life, vacations, and retirement, and he is open to what you have to say as well.

You can see that he's in a place of growth in his life by what he is learning and sharing with you. He shares with you his plans without you having to ask or pry. Taking into consideration the obligations that you have to your family or career, he shares about how those obligations might shape your future planning together. You are a team in this situation in which both of your input is necessary to make decisions.

Promising Sign #5: You mutually respect one another. As you have been improving in asserting yourself to him, does he respond to you in a respectful manner? Respect is important for both of you to have with one another *equally* and is also *part of and enhances the deep friendship bond* that's so vital to the health of the relationship. You can grow to deeply love someone you respect, but can you really love someone in a healthy way if you feel little respect for that person? Probably not.

Respect is also associated with good communication, which we have discussed in the previous chapter. If your partner treats you with respect and communicates to you in a respectful manner, and you do the same for him, you have a solid base for the relationship to grow upon. Respect is also inherent in these six promising signs that we are discussing.

Promising Sign #6: You each take responsibility for where you are. This promising sign is also associated with the good communication skills you've been practicing. It prevents defensiveness from taking over in the relationship. If you can each see the parts that you play in the problems that come between you, you'll be able take quicker steps to work through the issues at hand.

It's okay if he (and you) make mistakes or have arguments in the relationship. If both of you can acknowledge your parts when a breakdown in communication occurs, it will help you both to feel more secure with one another – and this is a good sign. The openness involved in listening and validating your partner's feelings even when you don't agree promotes the acceptance of differences and giving each other a break – important factors in a "hold 'em" relationship. There's a great deal of relief and comfort that exists between two people when they can each say, "I realize how what I've done affects you." It's important to look, with curiosity, for the good intentions behind what looks like "bad" behavior.

In regards to the status of your relationship, you can both acknowledge the following: yes, he is still "with her," but you are still "with him" as well. You are part of the picture! It'll be up to *him* to execute his plan with timeliness AND it is up to *you* to accept the fact that you are currently staying by choice *until you decide otherwise*. (If you are being held by force, please call 911 before reading on!)

Debriefing The Signs

If you can *really see evidence* of your partner achieving these promising signs, then you might want to "hold 'em." If he has already made *concrete actions* towards some of these steps, then that's a promising sign in and of itself.

As you know, we advocate your taking responsibility for your part in how the relationship goes. The good news is that, as you've been "working the program," you've indirectly changed the dynamic of your relationship! In turn, your partner may have become *more* motivated to do his part to make changes *in response to your changes*. Did he?

At this time, your partner may meet some of the promising signs while falling short on some of the others. You might be feeling confused and unsure right now. Or, perhaps he really does not show these signs at all ... you might want to throw this book out the window! But wait a minute. As we discussed in Chapter Two, even if your partner is not fully "Mr. Ready," it does not mean that he never will be. *Only you can decide how long of a time period is acceptable to wait for him.*

In the next chapter, we identify the red flags that may be telling you it's time to let go and "fold 'em." This may be challenging to do. If this is the path you'll be taking, we'll make it easier along the way in the remaining chapters.

12

Knowing When to Fold 'Em: Identifying the red flags that may be telling you it's time to let go!

Disclaimer: (Have you skipped ahead to this chapter in order to get some clear answers? This chapter will benefit you most after you've completed the exercises we've recommended along with evaluating how things have progressed in your relationship).

The Unhealthy Relationship

You've invested physically, mentally, and emotionally into this relationship. Together in this program, we have gone far! Still, it can be challenging to observe your relationship *as it truly is*. Your love and investment make it hard to decipher *what could be and what actually is.* Whether it's time to let go of him … or at least the dream you have with him.

Isn't it so much easier to give the best advice to *others* than to *ourselves*? The truth is, the more hooked we are in a situation, the cloudier our focus becomes. It becomes more difficult to see the flags from the fog. The process can be even harder if he knows *"just what to say"* in the moment to calm your fears.

All the cards are on the table now. So, it's important to stay focused and take good care of *yourself*. The more information you have, the better able you will be to make choices that are good for you. Good, not only in the current moment, but for what really matters in your life.

In the game of poker, a clear assessment of the cards in play is key to success. The cards determine whether you keep buying in or cash out. This chapter will provide you with more information about which cards may or may not be in play in your relationship!

There are two general unsavory factors that *contribute* to the demise of relationships. The stress of your situation makes the two of you vulnerable to these factors showing up! They relate to the level of *respect* in the relationship. Ask yourself if you've noticed the following problems as you've been working this program.

The Critical Charlie

How do you and your partner speak to each other? Has it gotten to the point where either of you speak with a *"what's-wrong-with-you"* tone? An example of this would be, "You *always* cry when you get upset!" Critical Charlie can generally live in either of you. Critical Charlie can arise in you from too many hurts and not enough understanding. It can arise in him if he is annoyed about your needs. Regardless, if Critical Charlie is on the scene, you're holding a tough hand.

The Scornful Scotty

You know Scornful Scotty has arrived when you or your partner are showing *disrespect, disdain, and general dislike*. Scornful Scotty says things like, "You're not *capable* of comprehending what I'm going through!" Over time, acting like a Scotty will sow seeds of anger and resentment. This will destroy the garden you are trying to grow. You and your partner will go into your separate corners in lieu of working together.

Critical Charlie and Scornful Scotty are poison to any relationship! The necessary trust and closeness needed cannot thrive when they're around. Keep this in mind while you review the following red flags. These factors will add fuel to the fires identified in the red flags below.

Red Flag #1: He is not taking any concrete steps to leave his wife. "No, duh!" you might say. This seems to be an obvious one. But, it may not be apparent if your partner is in a place of avoidance. He might be talking the talk but *not* walking the walk! *Your partner might ease your mind by telling you what you want and need to hear.* However, when it comes right down to it, is he taking action or not? Can you see it? If he's telling you that he *is*, is he being honest with you?

As we mentioned in the previous chapter about the first promising sign, transparency between the two of you is the best indicator that he's being honest with you. You might wonder how you can *really know* if he's being honest. Does he guard his phone, computer, or emails like he's an international spy? Does he use Snap Chat or other apps that can easily erase his texting history? Is he defensive when you want to look at his phone? If he's not transparent, this is a red flag! He may turn it around on you and say, "I want you to trust me." But, if he has nothing to hide ... then why the hiding behaviors?

Red Flag #2: Lagging! Pushing back his "deadlines." There always seems to be a "good reason" (i.e., excuse) for him to push back his deadlines. If he's avoiding official separation, divorce, or telling his family what's going on, he *still* may have "*reasons.*"

Nonetheless, these reasons affect *your* life greatly. Had he originally promised you that he would move on by a certain time? Has that time long since passed? If so, this is reason for concern. As in poker, do you finally need to call his bluff? For example, you could say, "Okay, I will accept your new timeline if you agree to let me speak to your wife in person if you still haven't done it by then."

This is why we have encouraged you to set *your own* timeline. If his timeline hasn't been reliable, then you've got the security of your own! What is in your control? It is certainly not him. He has made you aware of that through his behavior. You do have control over your boundaries, limits, and timeline.

His reasons for pushing back his deadlines may *seem* solid and well-intentioned. Let's say that something unfortunate happened "right before" he was planning to move out. For example, his wife was diagnosed with an illness. Maybe his child developed behavioral problems. You might think, "Well, he has to spend more time with his family right now." And that he might think you're selfish to hold him to his timeline. The bottom line is, he has to show his seriousness about moving on with you. Mr. Ready knows that family stressors will *always be there*, whether he sticks to his deadlines or not.

Red Flag #3: It's a closet romance. It's understandable if your partner wanted to be discrete with you at the beginning of the relationship (before his feelings became as strong as they are now). But are you still a complete secret? Can you only be seen in public together out of town, on vacation, or hardly ever at all? If so, then you are literally still being kept in the dark.

Would it be a complete surprise to his family and friends that he's been seeing you? If so, he's still trying to maintain an image of having a solid marriage. If his self-image is directly related to what others in his world think of him, he'll be more motivated to lead a double life. Keeping a secret life with you makes things easier for him in the long run (or so he believes).

If you are still in the dark about *his* life, a lightbulb should be going on! There should be no privacy here. Openness and transparency are in order at this stage. Do you not know where he lives? Have you ever been allowed to see his home, even briefly? Do you barely know anything about his work or friends? These are clear indicators of just how separated from his real life you really are. If you have asked to be more clued in but have been met with avoidance or push-back, he's wrapping himself up in a bright red flag!

Red Flag #4: He is staying with his wife for "the sake of the children or money." Is his motivation for staying married still either of these reasons? If so, then he's clearly showing that these factors take priority over his happiness with you. It's not likely this red flag would change any time soon. This is especially true if he fears a significant change in lifestyle or guilt about affecting his children with a divorce.

It's very common for parents to think that a divorce would "damage" their children. However, researchers have shown that children are very resilient and can get over a divorce within a few years. Nonetheless, he may not want to deal with what he can't control in a divorce. He may worry that he would have less control over what their mother says about him or who may come into their lives. In the same vein, he may not want a court to control what he is required to pay in alimony and/or child support. Even though he wants to be with you, if he has great difficulty coming to terms with these factors, you might be waiting a very long time.

Red Flag #5: You feel more heartache than happiness. A healthy relationship is one in which you and your partner feel secure together. When your relationship is not your "safe place," as a couple, you hit the wall. The relationship is stuck! Your ability to develop a deeper sense of joy is hindered. This pain often slithers into other areas of your life. When you notice that you're feeling more hurt than happy, you're holding onto more of what *could be* than what *is*.

When you're hurting, does it feel like you *hate* him for what he's "doing to you"? When you come together during the "good times," does the hate melt away? Doesn't it only come back again the next time you are triggered? You may find yourself trying to cover up the pain and worry when you're with him, not wanting to "ruin the mood" or "sabotage things."

You might think that he's doing you wrong. If so, there's a righteous anger that keeps you in a place of anguish. However, as we mentioned, there are parts of this relationship picture *for which you are also responsible*. You can still help *yourself* in this situation even when you think *he owes you*. This red flag is probably the most painful one, yet it's also the one you can take some charge over, *for your own sake*.

Red Flag #6: The main thing you have in common is sex. Really think about this one. This one might be hard for you to admit if it's true. He might be a good listener and make you *think* you have a lot in common. Especially if he validates your thoughts, opinions, hobbies, and lifestyle.

What if sex was taken out of your relationship? Would you have things to talk about? Do you have similar values, viewpoints, and interests? Are there interests that are important to you both, even if your personalities differ? Although being attracted to your partner and having a healthy sex life are important, the deep friendship connection is paramount to long-term success. If this best-friendship simply isn't there, but the sexual connection is, you might be hard-pressed to hope this will ultimately change.

Excuses vs. Information

Have you been able to acknowledge that some (or all) of these red flags still exist in your relationship? Even after all your hard work, you may not be sure what you want to do about them. If so, what more information do you need to make your decision about accepting or going? It will be up to you to decide if you can truly be at peace with a lack of a decision and more of the same. Is there any more information you need to make the decision that will be best for you in the long run? If so, it's important to identify this and use the tools we have discussed to obtain this.

As we mentioned in Chapter Four, not making a decision is still a decision! You may decide to adjust your timeline again. Or, deciding to "not decide until _____ time." This may feel more purposeful to you because it is a *decision*. In most cases though, you likely have the information you need. *If you cannot think of what information you may still need, and many of these red flags are present, you may be making excuses! Excuses can keep you from the pain of mourning a break-up.* If this is the case, "protecting yourself" is at the cost of keeping you stuck. You can have a healthy relationship, it just may not be with him.

Excuses are truly a response to fear. What would life be like if you let go of the relationship? Do you lack the confidence that you could cope with the grieving process that would follow? You may be having trouble letting in the truth; facing the flags means the relationship has run its course. It does not mean that a break up would be your failure on a personal level.

Not wanting to feel like "a failure" may make one actually "fail" by drifting away from one's *true* relationship goals. You may be stuck in a relationship in which your goals are not achievable (with him) because they take two! If you find yourself explaining away the red flags, the main issue at the forefront may be your difficulty in accepting the facts of *what you have seen*. It's a hard pill to swallow that you might have to *move forward without him* to reach your true goals.

STEP FOUR

Final Round - Putting Uncertainty in the Past

13

Moving on Together: Allowing the relationship to flourish in the best way possible.

So It All Worked Out? Great! What's Next ...

This chapter starts off with the assumption that the end result of all your hard work on this relationship has yielded what you've wanted all along: you and your partner, really together.

Have you *not* been heading towards this outcome during the course of reading this book? Is your relationship coming to a close? If so, skip ahead to the next chapter where we'll assist you in moving on apart. Although moving on apart may seem like yet another uphill battle, you can get through it, and you will. Just as you've applied skills and techniques so far, you can also do so in closing this particular chapter in life.

If your relationship *has* succeeded, *despite* its challenges, now you can focus on moving on together! Certainly, some of the same triggers are bound to pop up again. Old wounds, sensitive topics, his ex-wife, finances, and his kids are part of the picture. It stands to reason that being together doesn't necessarily come along with constant peace and harmony. Even in the strongest of relationships, some issues simply never get resolved.

Moving on together, it's crucial for you to avoid harping on the past! If you've been communicating assertively with him, he knows what he needs to do to help you feel safe. Focusing on the past is akin to complaining, guilt-tripping, and just plain nagging. It will not help *him* feel safe.

The dynamics of the relationship will likely change, if they haven't already! In other words, as the *mystery* decreases and the *safety* increases, so will your bond. The "healthy" response to this change would be that the bond would become stronger. The "unhealthy" response would be that the bond would become shaky and unstable. The bond would be *disrupted* by peace and tranquility, as ironic as that sounds.

Remember when we discussed the different types of connections in Chapter Three? To re-cap, if you're accustomed to "unhealthy" ways of connecting, being "too close" makes you uncomfortable. The newfound safety in your relationship may disturb you to the point where you create distance. This is a problematic relational dynamic we're about to explore a bit further.

Creating Distance: The Push/Pull

We've noticed a common dynamic in most all relationships. We call it the "push/pull." This dynamic exists in order to create *emotional* distance in a relationship. You might wonder how or why this happens. Shouldn't partners want to feel close? Why would they create distance with one another?

The desire to create distance and the push/pull dynamic are entirely unconscious. The people who do it are not aware they're doing it! The "push" consists of Partner A coming *towards* Partner B. The "pull" consists of Partner B *pulling away* as a result. When

Partner B feels guilty about pulling away or has had enough distance, he or she then comes towards Partner A, who now pulls away in turn. It goes on, with both partners engaging in the process.

Does this concept seem confusing? Consider the following. *Have you ever noticed that you were more physically attracted to someone who seemed cold or distant than someone who treated you kindly and with affection? Have you ever noticed that you found yourself getting annoyed with the person who treated you warmly and affectionately, while craving attention from the person who was cold and distant?*

Maybe you haven't experienced this for yourself. Perhaps you've witnessed a close friend go through this type of dynamic? It's the same concept as "the thrill of the chase"! *This is classic push/pull in action!*

Let's put push/pull in an even bigger perspective. We've noticed a common complaint while working with many single women: "There are no good guys! All the good ones are taken! I want a good guy!" Do they *really* want a good guy? Or, could their earlier experiences be telling them that the more difficult it is to get his love, the more satisfying and worthwhile it will be. When a "good guy" comes around, how does she really feel toward him? *She'll often report that she feels no chemistry and she "just doesn't feel the spark."*

Does this sound familiar? If this is a theme, you may be attracted to men who are emotionally unavailable. This is another example of classic push/pull playing out in the bigger picture.

Linda noticed the push/pull in her own relationship with Michael and brought it to our attention, as it had perplexed her. "Sometimes when Michael treats me really nice and loving, like when we have a nice weekend together, and he is more affectionate with me than usual, I end up picking a fight with him. About silly things, I don't even remember what they are. He pointed it out to me and it's true. Then he pulls away and I feel bad, and then I become the loving, affectionate one … on my own terms."

A desire for closeness while at the same time being uncomfortable with emotional intimacy is the main reason people engage in push/pull. Due to connection issues that spring from childhood, which we outlined in Chapter Three, it becomes a safety mechanism to repeat the dysfunctional dynamics of the past. Those dynamics are *familiar* and it feels safer to have a certain amount of distance. Closeness is new and sometimes frightening.

Don't worry; push/pull doesn't have to damage your relationship! It'll benefit you both to be aware of it and resist the urge to give in to it. However, it can be quite harmful if not addressed.

Being able to recognize and acknowledge when it shows up will allow both of you to have "higher-level discussions" rather than "common arguments." Instead of arguing about surface topics that come up and agitate the both of you, you can have enlightened discussions about the *way* you both interact with one another, the *process* that takes place between you rather than the small details that mask what's really going on.

How To Handle The Kids

Another test of your relationship lies in being a "united team" before the children. If you and your partner don't have children, skip forward to the next section about trust. If there are children in the picture, no matter their age, they'll be a factor. A comprehensive guide to co-parenting is outside the scope of this book. We do, however, make some points that we believe are salient to your situation.

Handling The Kids 101:

- Allow time for the kids to adjust to the new dynamic.
- Allow the kids to feel hurt.
- Allow them to *not be like you* (and to not feel excited about the new changes).
- Kids have difficulty with too many changes at once. Do not take this personally.
- Listen. Praise good behaviors. Do things on their level when possible.
- With your partner, do set family rules, chores, and discipline.

- Do your best to divide attention equally between all family members.

- You will have to "share" him with his kids.

- Be respectful and understanding.

The adjustment might be difficult and put a strain on the family. If this is the case, you and your partner might consider family therapy. Family therapy including the kids can help ease the transition. We recommend finding a therapist with specific training in both Cognitive Behavioral Therapy and Family Therapy modalities.

His Kids

His kids may or may not know the truth of your relationship and its beginnings. Whether his kids are young or fully-grown, they don't need to know the details. You and your partner are to decide *together* what's appropriate for them to know.

Their mother may have already told them things that you wanted to keep private. For example, if they know their father was in a relationship with you while still married, they may carry resentment and anger. Unfortunately, the large target of those negative feelings will be you. This part, however, may just simply come with the territory.

Such challenges can be overcome by the way you and your partner present yourselves, as a team! Do you want a household environment that encourages respect as a family value? You both will need to "model" respectful behavior to one another and the kids.

Also, allow the kids to *change* in the way they relate to you! Things might start out rocky and equalize over time. It might take a brief amount of time for them to warm up to you or it might take years. Let them have their feelings. When they're ready to accept you, they will. This part might be challenging for you, so we encourage you to take a "bigger-picture" perspective here. Try not to take their attitude toward you personally. (Unless you can admit if there were times you were unfair or hurtful to them as well. If this is the case, you might consider approaching them, offering a genuine apology, and asking for forgiveness. This is warranted if you have hurt or wronged them directly).

Your Kids

The same information goes for your children as well. They're adjusting to a new dynamic, particularly if they've had you all to themselves. If they aren't accepting your partner (or even that you have a partner at all), it's all the more important to model respect. You and your partner do this together, as "teammates."

We appreciate how challenging it can be to assert yourself with your kids. It can be especially difficult if you've been a single parent in the role of a sort of "friend." Does this sound familiar? You may have done this, whether consciously or not. Now it's time to take on a clear "parent" role.

Rest assured, though, that children are more resilient than they are given credit for. They will adjust to the new dynamic. You can help them adjust by setting the new boundaries in a kind and loving manner. Changes made in sudden and shocking ways will confuse them.

If your children take issue with your partner, for whatever reason, it's appropriate to listen to their grievances. Validate their feelings when you can. Review your listening skills from Chapter Seven. Practice the Reflection and Validation skills. Oftentimes, that's all it takes for them to know that you've taken in what they've said. They have the right to their feelings. When they express their feelings to you, you don't need to change your feelings based on theirs.

Trust, But Verify

This section is about fostering continued trust in the next chapters of your relationship. We encourage you to trust one another while also simply knowing that there are no guarantees in life. This is a double-edged sword that we all must live with! It's in our best interest to trust the people closest to us. But we can still be aware that we can never be 100% sure about anything.

How frustrating, you might think! After all this, how dare we tell you not to have 100% certainty in your relationship?

We don't want this truth to *dominate* your relationship. It's simply a statement speaking to the lack of *absolute* certainty in any situation. It need not be given any more thought than this section.

This is the reason that "trust, but verify" is so useful. You should both be able to do this without becoming defensive. This is used within your relationship whenever either of you need to just "make sure" that things are kosher between the two of you.

For example, "trust, but verify" might include checking your partner's phone at random or having him check yours. We commonly tell clients that if there's nothing to hide, on either side, then it isn't a big deal! There's nothing wrong with you and/or your partner needing reassurance from time to time.

Getting the reassurance you need from an occasional "trust, but verify" action also helps to foster the sense of safety in your relationship. Now that you have both moved on together, you deserve to feel safe with one another. Dealing with any doubts or fears that stand in the way of you becoming even closer is ultimately helpful.

Summary

Moving on together is a big milestone! We've highlighted some of the important things to keep in mind now. The "push/pull" dynamic might show up now that your relationship has changed for the better. The more "available" you are to one another, the more likely it may show up! Learning how to openly deal with this paradoxical dynamic will help you both get even closer. Additionally, we've covered some pointers in dealing with his and your kids. We recommend family therapy if problems persist or worsen. Lastly, we mentioned "trust, but verify" as a good way to help you both continue to feel safe with each other.

In the next chapter, we help you move on apart if this is the case for you. The good news is that you've already been building your muscle for this transition.

14

Moving on Apart

"I think it's unfair, but they have the right as fallible, screwed-up humans to be unfair; that's the human condition." -Albert Ellis

It's Run Its Course

This chapter starts with the assumption that your relationship is now in the process of ending. Significant break-ups can often lead to full-blown grief reactions. The process registers in the brain similarly to mourning a loved one's death. As such, we recognize the need to assist you with this process. We take into consideration all you've put into this relationship and all the knowledge you've gained along the way.

Is your relationship ending because you or your partner has consciously made this final decision? Or has it "run its course" with a power of its own, leading itself to its demise?

Either way, we encourage you to take this time to ground yourself! Right now, you may feel like hiding under the covers or distracting yourself with non-stop activities. We encourage a more straight-forward approach to better prepare you for the final stages!

You Need a Plan

If you are the one who is ending this relationship, finally and certainly, you'll need a plan. A plan will help you execute a break up in no uncertain terms.

Have you already attempted to end this relationship in the past only to get sucked in again by his charming ways, reminding you of the things you love about him? If you know this relationship *needs to end, for your sake*, a concrete plan of action will guide you. We've outlined some main points to consider.

When communicating to him that the relationship has run its course, we encourage you to pick a public spot where you feel comfortable. That way, you can leave when you're finished. It may seem awkward to have this conversation in public! But, a public setting helps to keep the meeting structured and contained. Also, you'll less likely be "maneuvered" out of your decision in a public place.

What time of day or evening do you want to execute your plan? Timing is important! We recommend having specific plans and a comfortable, nurturing place to go afterward. Make it a short-term conversation; do not allow it to drag out! At this point, you've likely both talked the future of your relationship into the ground. Re-hashing every point won't really help either of you if everything's already been said! Keeping the conversation brief and to-the-point shows him that you're moving forward and not pleading with him to change.

Having a place to go afterward holds you accountable. Tell a girlfriend about your plan and have her meet you at a different location. Follow through in making your meeting with him time-limited. Another benefit of meeting a close friend is that you start the moving-on process and avoid isolating yourself.

We also encourage you to send a clear message by using the communication skills you learned in Chapter Seven. Remember your template for assertive communication:

1. Describe the problem

2. Verbalize your feelings

3. State what you would like to see happen.

If the conversation becomes challenging and you receive push-back from him, you can utilize the "broken-record" technique. Simply repeat yourself and remember that you need not get side-tracked by the new points he brings up or the push-back you get. You can make sure the conversation stays on-topic. Point out to him that you don't want to get side-tracked from your main points. Be a broken-record if you need to be!

Example of "Break-Up Talk" Using Communication Skills from Chapter 7:

You: *(Setting up the discussion).* Thanks for coming here to meet me. I'm meeting Sandy for dinner so I only have a little bit of time. *(Describing the problem).* There hasn't been the amount of change that I've needed to continue to invest in this relationship. *(Verbalizing the feeling).* I am sad because this is no longer healthy for me. *(Stating what you would like to see happen).* What I want is for you to know that I am ending the relationship. I am moving on and I want you to understand and accept that.

Him: *(Invalidating).* Oh come on, I know you don't mean this. *(Side-tracking).* I will move out this weekend if it means that much to you!

You: *(Using Assertive Defense: first agreeing with what you can, then stating your position).* You may be promising more changes but as I said, I am moving on.

Him: *(Still trying to side-track you).* Just hang in there, give me some more time. I will do whatever I need to do.

You: (*Broken-Record Technique).* I understand that you are promising more changes but like I already said, I am going to move on.

We are aware that the above conversation can potentially go in many different directions. *But did you notice that it's possible to stick to your main points and your template for assertive communication despite any monkey wrench that gets thrown at you?* Be mindful that his *urgency* to get you to change your mind doesn't mean that you *must* change your mind.

We encourage you to practice by filling in the blanks below. You can anticipate how he will react and prepare your responses.

Practice:

Me: *(Set up the discussion with time limit).*

_____

(Describe the problem).

_____

(Verbalize the feeling).

_____

(State what I want).

_____

Him: *(What might he say?)*

_____

Me: *(Re-assert the point).*

_____

Him: *(How might he respond now?)*

_____

Me: *(Re-assert the point).*

_____

Making sure you stick with your good communication skills is challenging! We want to remind you that you can bring your notes or a cheat-sheet. Who says you can't refer to your notes to stay on track in the conversation? Use whatever resources you need to use in order to stay strong!

Your Artillery of Coping Skills to Combat "The Worries"

Remember learning about doing pleasurable tasks to improve your mood in Chapter Six? The same tasks can also be used as coping skills to help you get through this challenging time. Make efforts to avoid isolating yourself from family and friends. Staying active will give you continued purpose and structure, which is vital to a stable mood!

When your sadness turns into "the worries," you run into danger of going into another stuck-point in your life. You've just come out of one, no need to go back into another! "The worries" can lead you down a dark path of repeating situations and conversations with him in your mind. They will prevent you from being able to move on. Some people get so stuck in "the worries" that they spend hours re-hashing situations from the past that have disturbed them. They wind up getting upset for no reason at all!

If you think "the worries" are creeping up on you, ask yourself: "Are these 'the worries' or am I problem-solving?" If it's problem-solving, make a plan and write it out! If it's been three or more minutes and you haven't gotten anywhere with your thoughts, then it's "the worries"!

There's a simple intervention for this problem that will keep you from falling into a dark hole:

Step 1: Ask yourself, "Are these 'the worries' or am I actually problem-solving?"

Step 2: Recognize what's going on. Tell yourself, "Okay, 'the worries' have snuck up on me!"

Step 3: Make an *active decision* to re-focus onto something more pleasurable or to be more productive. Review your list of tasks from Chapter Six. Call a friend or family member you've been meaning to get in touch with, pay a bill you've been putting off, run some errands, check and sort through your mail, etc.

If "the worries" have you obsessing about things that *may or may not happen* in the future, we suggest keeping a worry log and writing them down! The best way to do this exercise is to exhaust your brain for at least 20 minutes by writing down: 1. What are you worried about? 2. What do you think will happen? 3. How will you cope? It may be challenging to exert energy on this task for 20 minutes, which is actually a good thing. Most people do not actually *want* to worry for a good 20 minutes straight. Go back to the log later: what *actually happened* and how did you cope?

The bottom line: there's no point in painstakingly stewing on every aspect of the relationship. Focusing on all the times you felt hurt and confused, all the times he was unfair to you, and why it didn't work out even though you tried will not help you. It's advisable, though, to reflect *generally* upon the relationship *for the purpose of learning from this experience*, as we discuss in the next section.

Your (and His) Contributions

You both contributed strengths and weaknesses that made up the fabric of the relationship. It didn't exist in a vacuum. Both of you brought forth things that enhanced the relationship while both of you contributed to the cracks in the foundation.

It may be tempting to blame him alone for the reasons the relationship ended. It's easier to see your contributions in a positive light and his in a negative one. Of course, if the relationship ended because he ultimately didn't keep his promises to you or he left you entirely, then the *immediate* "fault" lies with him. He didn't follow through as you thought he would.

However, the "contributions" of both of you lie deeper than the immediate "fault"! They include the ways you interacted together, the ways you treated one another. These things are worthy of examining, in a neutral way, without assigning blame. As we've already mentioned, *there really is no fault because there really is no failing.*

A good way to enhance your learning, if you want to go a step beyond simply reflecting, is to engage in some journaling. Journaling, if done properly, can be an excellent way to cope, heal, and learn from this experience. Journaling is *not* be helpful when it's done as a stream-of-consciousness, angry rant. Ranting will only help you *practice* feeling hurt and angry.

Guide to Constructive Journaling

Processing in your journal what you did, did not do, or could have done better can help you "file away" past events. Being honest with yourself is the only way you'll really learn from this experience. Infuse empathy for yourself over the things for which you had no control or responsibility.

Imagine yourself outside of your body as you journal. Imagine that you're observing yourself in the relationship, gliding like a bird over you and him as it unfolded. Consider incorporating the following points while you journal for a better ability to understand, let go, and begin the healing process:

1. Describe the facts of what occurred in the relationship.

2. What events, images, and situations are difficult for me to let go of?

3. In what ways have I been hurt by him and by myself?

4. How could I handle things differently or better in the future?

5. What learning can I now bring into my future relationships?

6. How have I been strong in the past during times of emotional hardship and how can those strengths help me during this challenging time?

How Did This All Happen? ... Making Sense of It All

If you're engaging in the constructive journaling, you're already moving towards making sense of it all in a way that benefits you in the long run! You are learning about yourself in a deep way. You are realizing that you can take away many new lessons from the relationship that you might not have otherwise learned in your life. Even if your head is spinning in the aftermath, being able to figure out what you can learn from the experience will help you stay grounded.

In Chapter Three, we examined the childhood struggles that may have led you to attach to someone who was not readily available to you. Have you been scratching your head and wondering how this all happened to you? If so, we recommend reviewing the section in Chapter Three about connection styles.

Do you relate to the anxious connection style? Circumstances around your upbringing may have allowed you to feel safer when there was some distance between yourself and your primary caretakers. Thus, in your adult life, you would likely seek out partners who are not available to you, as the distance and difficulty approaching him would help you feel more safe and comfortable.

Along those lines, you would also feel more comfortable having control over when and how your partner would be able to *come to you*. It might be a relief to you to keep him at arm's length and only allow him "in" when it *works for you*, when the circumstances are in your control.

It'll be up to you to decide whether or not you prefer to keep your learned connecting style. You might want to trade it in for a new one: the confident connection! In the confident connection style, you feel safe and comfortable with closeness. You don't feel the need to create the push/pull dynamic and pull away from your partner. Closeness does not frighten you or turn you off. The confident connection style also allows you to feel comfortable when there is reasonable distance between you and your partner (so long as the distance has not been created as part of the push/pull dynamic.)

Summary

If your relationship has come to its final stages, we've helped you design a plan to break it off in a final way so that you can move on in your life. You are prepared to deal with challenging emotions by putting your coping skills into practice. You know how to manage "the worries," which will only serve to drag you down. You've realized that you can make the best of this chapter in your life by learning important lessons about yourself. By reflecting back on your connecting style, you've also recognized that, although you cannot change the *events* of your childhood, you can choose to change your connecting style from now on.

15

Letting Go and Moving Forward

"It is better to conquer yourself than to win a thousand battles. Then the victory is yours. It cannot be taken from you, not by angels or by demons, heaven or hell." -Buddha

How Long Till I Heal?

There's an unfortunate stereotype about women that they tend to become "bitter" and "angry" when their relationships don't work out. What the critics don't know is that the anger doesn't just come out of nowhere! Anger happens when we think it's unfair that our partner didn't do what they "should have." The truth is that people (and life in general) are fair ... sometimes!

Beneath anger is hurt and fear. The hurt makes logical sense. You may be thinking that he didn't have enough love for you in order to choose the relationship. The fear is also understandable.

You may now question whether you'll be able to find a wonderful partner.

There's no right or wrong time to "stop" hurting. The pain can ebb and flow for a while. But that just means you'll need to work extra hard to take care of yourself. Balancing your life and making sure to connect with comforting friends or family members will help.

If you're feeling intense emotions such as anger, rage, shame, and/or depression, you might be tempted to stew in those emotions! Are you plotting revenge or feeling sorry for yourself? As convincing as those emotions might be in tempting you to dwell, doing so will only bring you further down a dark hole.

The following can set you on a healthy road to healing:

- *Understand "Hurt" As "Learning"*

Since the time of the ancient Greeks, pain and suffering were seen as necessary for knowledge. Eastern philosophies viewed being apart from loved ones as a *form of mental suffering necessary for happiness.* Suffering and happiness are parts of life that are *not permanent.* Accepting the suffering of detachment while re-attaching to yourself and others are necessary to lift the pain.

- *Beware The Shoulds*

Though pain and suffering are not thoughts, they *connect* to thoughts. If you look, you'll see many "shoulds" that lurk behind your pain: "This *should not* have happened to me," "He *should not* have hurt me like this," "I *should* have known better." But where in the world does it say that these types of situations, although painful to bear, *should not* happen and *therefore must not* happen? It certainly would have been nice if the relationship had worked out. *But there is no written rule that it should have.*

Awareness of the "shoulds" and "musts" *will help set you free.* If you're able to *recognize the desire and wish* for what you wanted while *refusing* to turn that desire into *an absolute of what "should have been,"* you can start the process of really healing! Accepting the true reality of the end of a chapter (if you allow it to be) will help you let go of anger or resentment of what *would have been nice and desirable* so you can begin anew.

- *How we Feel Helps How we Heal*

Have you noticed the ebbs and flows of your grief? Perhaps in the morning or at night the situation seems more hopeless? Then, during the day at work or with friends you feel more hopeful? How you feel connects to the lens through which you view your situation. The waves of negative emotion will come and go. This is part of the grieving process. Noticing the times when you're more hopeful provides *important information* on what's *helping* you feel more hopeful!

- *Practice Seeing You – Strengthening What is True!*

Hurt, pain, and the "shoulds" and "musts" that follow can negatively affect the way you see yourself. The end of the relationship can trigger older feelings of loss or abandonment. Old beliefs about your worth, value, and lovability can lead to self-doubt. This ultimately prolongs the healing process.

All people have a continuum of how they see themselves. For example, it's common to see oneself as worthless or unlovable (or both) while in the throes of emotional pain. It's also common to see oneself as valuable and lovable while experiencing happiness. Your *mood* can influence how you *judge yourself as a person*! Don't trust your opinions of yourself while you're feeling down!

Do you see yourself as worthless or unlovable following this break up? How would you rather see yourself instead? If you want to see yourself as lovable, get out of your head and think of a close friend! What are the qualities that make your friend lovable?

Linda struggled with feeling quite unlovable when Michael continued to avoid following through on his promises. Their relationship ultimately ended. Linda identified that even though she felt 100% *unlovable*, she saw her friend Karen as *lovable* because Karen was kind, responsible, ambitious, smart, and nice to be around. While learning about the concept of "lovable" existing on a *continuum*, Linda rated Karen on a scale of 1 - 100% as: Kind (90%), Responsible (75%), Ambitious (55%), Smart (80%), and Nice to be around (90%).

So, what percent are *you* lovable or _____ (*insert the quality you want to target*)? A good way to build this true positive outlook is to look (on a daily basis) for the ways that you are kind, responsible, ambitious, smart, or nice to be around. You can use these adjectives if they resonate for you or better yet, create your own. On a daily basis, if you write down 2-3 small pieces of evidence for lovable or _____, you'll stay focused on what is *true*! This is more useful than letting your *mood* dictate how you see yourself!

- *Stand Balanced*

How you eat, sleep, work, engage with people, and spend your alone time all relate to your own sense of personal balance. "Striving for balance" is a principle discussed throughout history!

According to Buddhism and Islam, there is the principle of the "middle way." In Confucianism, there is the "doctrine of the mean." In Taoism, there is the "balance between yin and yang" and in Hinduism, there is the concept of "balancing the chakras." In modern Cognitive Behavioral Therapy, "balance" is the process of designing life in such a way that accomplishment tasks, anti-avoidance tasks, and pleasurable activities co-exist in harmony!

To Forgive or Not To Forgive?

Many books have been written about the importance of forgiveness. It's often described as an important part of the healing process. It would be nice if one could simply "choose" to forgive. But, it's not as easy as it sounds. Are there benefits to granting forgiveness? Yes. Must you forgive him for hurting you in order to move on in your life? No. Let's explore what's best for you.

Abrahms-Spring challenges the common notion that forgiveness must occur in order to move on in a healthy way. She writes that a different process, Acceptance, can occur instead when forgiveness is not possible.

Experts on forgiveness have maintained that the offender must first ask for forgiveness. That he "must make efforts to correct his wrongs" in order for *true* forgiveness to take place. But in your case, how realistic is this? Do you imagine him making such efforts without wanting anything in return? If he hadn't followed through on his part and hadn't done what was "required of him," then how can you truly forgive? If you need him to come to you and really "understand your pain" you can get stuck, if this is what you're basing your forgiveness upon.

A common error when thinking about forgiveness may be holding you back. People often believe that once they decide to forgive, they must do so in an *all-or-nothing* way. As though forgiveness is like donating blood, you must do it fully, in large quantities, if you decide to do it at all. Actually, it can be granted in small doses, over a period of time. You can set the pace that feels right for you. Maybe you can start by *partially* forgiving. Or, you can decide to forgive certain actions and not others. It need not be the grand gesture that it is sometimes portrayed to be.

We see forgiveness as an ongoing process that you may or may not choose to do. It can occur regardless of whether he has acknowledged the pain he has caused. His lack of acknowledgement or apology does not need to hold you back from the process of letting go. Don't forgive because it's the *"right thing to do."* Make forgiving part of your personal healing process if you decide it's better for you.

A Neutral Space

Does the idea of forgiving him seem to be outside of the realm of possibility? If so, we encourage you to exist in what we call The Neutral Space. The Neutral Space is a frame of mind in which you see him as neither good nor bad. It is accepting that he is simply a fallible human, as we all are. Our concern is that if you see him as a completely "bad person," you will remain stuck in anger. This will make it all the more difficult for you to move forward. Yes, many of the things he did or still does may very well be downright wrong. But those are his *actions* that have hurt you, not his essence as a human. To be "bad," there would be no good actions that he does, ever.

You may find that your brain is going back and forth over him. There may be moments when you wake up and your brain reminds you of all the good memories and things about him that you miss. You may then feel a yearning and loneliness for him. At other times, you may be reminded of the hurts and betrayal that you experienced. This may lead you to feel anger and resentment toward him. Basically, your brain is trying to process this loss. But how can you make sense of it all when two extremes exist in your memory? "He was the man of my dreams and then, all of a sudden, he became the Devil incarnate!"

You can help your brain fully process this once you're able to build a bridge between the "good" and the "bad." When your brain brings you an image of the good, you can also connect it with one of the more difficult memories. For example, "I miss when we went away on overnights, but I don't miss never knowing when he would be free again." Connecting the good and the bad lets your brain process who he really is: imperfect and not healthy for you.

Being in The Neutral Space gives you relief from these extreme ways of thinking and feeling. Think about when people in your life have done things that hurt you. Suppose you and your best friend had a falling out during a certain period or suppose your child said something very mean and nasty to you in a fit of rage that seemed to cut your heart. Would you consider these people as "bad" or "evil" to the core? We would think probably not. You would most likely be able to see that it had been their *actions* that had hurt you and not necessarily *who they were as people.*

The Neutral Space also allows for the possibility of forgiveness at a later time. When you think more flexibly, you won't get stuck by making rigid decisions or predictions about how you will feel in the future. You allow your feelings to evolve and change over time.

New Me

As you reflect on this relationship, what are the lessons that you've learned? You *can* see these lessons as an opportunity to learn and grow. Consider the changes you want to make as you move forward. Will you have less of a tolerance for an unavailable man in the future? Can you imagine noticing the red flags earlier and managing your reactions to them even better? If so, that means you are stronger now, even though it may not quite feel that way yet.

Now is a good time to see yourself as strengthening the newer you through practice. You already know some of your triggers when you were with him. How you dealt with those triggers can now be "old you" and how you will strive to respond in the future will be the "new you." This work in progress can continue to evolve like a fine wine. The way you handle your relationships moving forward will improve and be refined with practice.

When you decide, you can take what you've learned and continue your journey. The now-wiser you can design your path. You can make decisions such as whether to date casually or seriously. If you decide to date casually, you can create limits and boundaries. This will prevent you from getting emotionally attached until you're ready. For example, you can date more than one person at a time to keep from over-investing.

You may decide you'd rather be serious about your next partner. Regardless, we recommend making and sticking to a list of "Must-Have Values" that come from your learning. "Old you" may want you to compromise these values when another Mr. Charming comes to town. Still, "new you" knows you deserve to have the nurturing and committed relationship you desire.

Mr. Ready may not always be as *exciting* as Mr. Charming can be initially. But, deeper joy evolves from connecting your values to a Mr. Ready.

Values That Are Important to Share
– in my next relationship:

Personal:_____

Professional:_____

Family:_____

Spiritual: _____

Other Values: _____

Tip: Keep this list of values "close to you" by carrying it around in your wallet or writing it in the notes section on your phone. Reference the list frequently and use it as a future screening measure for potential new partners.

Conclusion: Relapse Prevention

This term is often used in the context of addictions but we find that it's appropriate in this context as well. Our hope for you is that you're standing so much stronger now than when you first started reading this book, you will have nowhere to go but forward! And even if you do find yourself in a similar relationship situation in the future, it won't be quite the same because you now have the tools you need to "prevent a relapse"! None of us are immune to relationship problems. But, if another Mr. Charming sneaks past your radar, you'll be better prepared.

You are your best investment and you certainly invested in yourself by reading this book and following this program. Let's recap the main points:

- You discovered, at the beginning of this book, the "type" of man you were with, which helped you to better understand his emotions and behaviors as well as give you a sense of how ready he had been to be with you.

- You learned about the ways you connected to your caregivers as a child, which influenced the ways that you currently connect to partners in adulthood. This helped you to make sense of how you got into this relationship from the very beginning. You can now be more easily aware of ways you might lapse into old ways of connecting.

- You set specific relational goals for yourself. This assisted you in "getting on track" with your partner. You can now post your goals moving forward in a place you will see them on a daily basis. Otherwise, time may lead you to forget what you've learned.

~ You learned how to manage anxiety by developing plans when attacked by the "What Ifs." The purpose of this was to better cope with anxiety by reinforcing your strengths and developing a plan. Moving forward, you can make it a point to continue your "What If/Then What" log to make sure worry does not lead you to future avoidance.

~ You mastered the art of keeping your mood balanced by engaging in pleasurable, anti-avoidance, and accomplishment tasks. This assisted you to be your best self in your relationship, focusing on you, and being less dependent upon him for your overall happiness. Moving forward, you can continue to find your balance on a daily basis to ensure your mood will stay strong.

~ You strengthened your communication skills, which also serves you in your next relationships going forward. The purpose of this was to develop assertiveness skills and continue to be your best self. You can continue to find ways to practice these skills with family or colleagues to make the skills a part of who you are now.

~ You set a timeline for yourself in order to honor the tolerance limit that you had. This helped you "stay on track" and to respect your own limits. You can continue to incorporate your revised timeline into your goals for the future. This will help you to keep your eyes on what you want.

~ You faced the avoidance that crept in which tried to trick you into a detour from your goals. You learned how to stay on course by fighting avoidance head-on. We didn't want you to slip past the hard work for too long! As you continue to strive for balance, you can be sure you are identifying and pushing through things that you may want to avoid. You will never regret taking steps that will make you better.

~ You identified how your partner took to all these changes and you were able to properly assess the results. This helped you come to some important conclusions about the future of your relationship and take control over your path. You can continue to practice assessing whether your relationships are in line with your values and making changes as needed.

~ You were able to keep moving forward in your life, whether you stayed with your partner or you ended your relationship. Learning about yourself while reflecting upon your contributions to the relationship has assisted in your plan to move forward.

~ All in all, you have gathered and practiced useful, concrete thinking, feeling, and behaving tools to help you as you heal. These tools will help you design a happier and healthier you.

Afterword

You've worked hard. We acknowledge what you've been through on this journey and we hope that you can ultimately take away much more from it than you would have thought possible before you read this book, for the sake of learning some valuable lessons. This book is the kind that, through multiple reads, will continue to give you more insights and help you strengthen your skills and resilience. Thank you for having invited us into this piece of your life experience.

References

Chapter 1 – Your situation

"Even in the field of self-help books" *After the affair.* e.g., Abrahms-Spring, J.; *Getting past the affair.* Snyder, D, Baucom, D & Gordon, K.

"Anxiety is a central part" DePompo, P. in Press.

Chapter 2 – His situation

"Married people who have affairs" *Is Infidelity a Cause or a Consequence of Poor Marital Quality?* Previti, D. & Amato, P.

"There are two prominent ideas" *Disarming the narcissist.* Behary, W.

Chapter 3 – How did I get here?

"How we connect in our adult romantic relationships" *Patterns of attachment: a psychological study of the strange situation.* Ainsworth, M.

Chapter 4 – Playing Your Cards Right

"It's no wonder that goal-focused people report psychological well-being" *Goal striving, needs satisfaction and longitudinal well-being: The self-concordance model.* Kennon & Elliot.

"A step to getting off the fence" *A selection from Benjamin Franklin's personal letters.* Franklin, B.

"One way to practice keeping your cool is by using mindfulness" *DBT skills training manual.* Linehan, M.

Chapter 5 – Tolerating the Uncertainty

"Your secret to winning the battle against the "What Ifs" is the development of … the "Then Whats!" *Personal Communication.* Padesky, C. & Mooney, K.

Chapter 6 – Taking Life Off-Hold

"Padesky's Five-Part Model shows this connection" *Mind over mood.* Padesky, C. & Greenberger, D.

"When you wait to "feel" like doing a task" *Overcoming depression one step at a time.* Martell, J.

Chapter 7 – Putting Yourself Out There

"Reflecting with reassurance helps the speaker to elaborate and open up more" *Active listening.* Rogers, C. & Farson.

Chapter 8 – Keeping You on Track – Seeing the Big Picture

"His failure to act is not a mystery" Depompo, P. In Press.

Chapter 9 – Facing Avoidance

"You will still have an interesting life" *How to make yourself happy and remarkably less disturbable.* Ellis, A.

Chapter 10 – Maintaining Your Focus

"Accepting the value difference helps you" DePompo, P. in Press.

Chapter 11 – Knowing When to Hold 'Em

"There are some misconceptions" *The seven principles for making marriage work.* Gottman, J.

"Six promising signs" DePompo, P. in Press.

Chapter 12 – Knowing When to Fold 'Em

"There are two general unsavory factors" *The seven principles for making marriage work.* Gottman, J.

"These factors will add fuel to the fires identified in the red flags below." DePompo, P. in Press.

Chapter 13 – Moving on Together

"Even in the strongest of relationships, some issues simply never get resolved" *The seven principles for making marriage work.* Gottman, J.

Chapter 14 – Moving on Apart

"Significant break-ups can often lead to full-blown grief reactions" *Reward, addiction, and emotion regulation systems associated with rejection in love.* Fisher, E., Brown, L., Strong, A & Mashek, D.

Chapter 15 – Letting Go and Moving Forward

"Beneath anger is hurt and fear" *Love is never enough.* Beck, A.

"Beware the shoulds" *A guide to rational living.* Ellis, A.

"Other Woman" Resources

Mental Health

Academy of Cognitive Therapy (ACT), www.AcademyofCT.org

Association for Behavioral and Cognitive Therapies (ABCT), www.abct.org

Anxiety and Depression Association of America (ADAA), www.adaa.org

The Infidelity Clinic, CBTI of Southern California, www.InfidelityClinic.com

National Alliance on Mental Illness (NAMI), www.nami.org

National Suicide Prevention Lifeline, (800) 273-8255

Moving On

Meet Up (neighbors getting together), www.meetup.com

Online Dating Reviews, http://www.consumersearch.com/online-dating

Made in the USA
Las Vegas, NV
27 July 2021